W

A sl

What If?
A shocking true story

ASMA PUMPI MOORE

❀ London 2004

Copyright © Asma Pumpi Moore 2004.
The right of Asma Pumpi Moore to be identified as author
of this work has been asserted by her in accordance with the
Copyright, Designs and Patents Act 1988.

Certain names have been changed to protect confidentiality.

Published in the UK 2004 by Pink Rose Press
707 High Road, London, N12 0BT
First published 2004 Trafford Publishers

All rights reserved.
No part of this publication may be reproduced or
transmitted in any form or by any means, electronic
or mechanical, including photocopy, recording or any
information storage and retrieval system, without
permission in writing from the publisher.

British Library Cataloguing Data
A catalogue record for this book is available
from the British Library.

Typeset in 10/13pt Minion by *typo*G, London
neil@typog.co.uk

Printed in the UK by Biddles, King's Lynn, Norfolk, PE30 4LS

*This book is dedicated to:
victims of domestic violence around the world;
my son Michael Sydney Moore (Mykey)
and
Sydney Michael Moore (woof, woof)*

ACKNOWLEDGMENTS

I WOULD LIKE TO EXPRESS my great gratitude to the Metropolitan Police officers, (who rescued me from the prison I was in).

Special thanks to my Chinese friend Lim, who gave strength and wisdom when I was a homeless and penniless girl. He practised what his religion, Buddhism, taught him.

I would like to thank my friend Michael Guest for all his kindness, and love for me and my little boy. Biggest thank you for Phuppo, for all her unconditional love.

I would also like to thank a few more people, whose love and affection will always live in my heart: Parrow, Liz, Rubina, Sawant, Azhar, Shani, Zain, Vikky, Zulfiqar, Raja, Tony Griffith, Laurence Joffe, Shinaz Patel, Tony McDonald and last but not least, Roddy Llewelyn.

I would like to thank my psychic, Shirley, for guiding and helping me for many years. Also my spiritual guide Michael Samuel Moore (Late).

A very special thanks for Javed Bhai, Aunt Kashvi and Aunt Fouzia for their kind help and great words of wisdom. And I am thankful for the lady in Brixton called Peggy, and her daughter Margaret.

I would like to thank my family, who are still on speaking terms despite what I did in the name of 'equality'.

I would also like to thank my teachers Dr Maureen Spencer, Mr Daniel Mokeyani, Dr Colin Francome and Mr Chis Cheng, at Middlesex University, for giving me help and encouragement during my law degree.

I do want to take this opportunity to thank Mrs Nora

Moore, (Carl's grandmother) and Sammy (Carl's uncle) and his family for standing by me, and their love and support for my son and me.

However, the biggest THANK YOU goes to my best friend – my son Mykey for his unconditional love and patience.

Asma Pumpi Moore
LONDON 2004

The Silent Screams

The thunder of silence
And the screams of solitude
Entering into a rampage of violence,
The sea is at peace
But the defences are weak
And the walls are trembling,
Is it the deep still sea
Keeping it quiet?
Or is it a volcano
Waiting to explode?

(APM)

CONTENTS

Chapter One:
The early training camp – 13

Chapter Two:
The emotional blackmail – 57

Chapter Three:
London 1986 – 99

Chapter Four:
Love, deceit and betrayal – 131

Chapter Five:
Domestic violence – 139

Chapter Six:
The police – 167

Chapter Seven:
Cul-de-sac – 173

Chapter Eight:
Sanity v insanity – 187

Chapter Nine
The end justifies the means – 205

INTRODUCTION

The wounds of my life have compelled me to open my heart in the form of a book.

The crusade of this book is to create awareness about the intensity of emotional extortion imposed by Asian parents on their daughters in an arranged marriage, in the name of religion; and the profound impact of domestic violence on victims and their children.

Thus, the book is divided into three parts:

1. The arranged marriage and the battle for freedom.
2. The love marriage and the domestic violence.
3. The lessons and the achievements.

I believe it is imperative to reach out to those women who are still in the emotional entrapment, and tell them that the key to the door of their freedom is in their own hands. To be able to find that key, they only have to unlock their minds!

So I see the mission of this book as threefold:

Firstly, it sheds light on certain grim Asian marriages, exposing the extent of male domination and degradation of women, and teaches young women to stand up for their rights.

Secondly, it addresses the universal problem of domestic violence and dysfunctional families amongst all people.

Thirdly, it suggests ways out of the apparent dead-end of an abusive marriage or relationship.

Author background

I was born and raised in Karachi, Pakistan, as one of seven children of a Syed family (the descendent of The Prophet Mohammed)

As I was the eldest of three daughters, it was imperative for my parents to make sure I followed the Islamic pattern.

My mother was the typical housewife of an Islamic household; her duties were restricted to producing and bringing up children, making sure they would follow the Islamic code, and obeying her "master", her husband, with an unquestioning obedience according to Islamic practice.

At birth I was too ill to be given a name: I was not expected to survive. An Italian friend of the family started calling me 'Pompeii', after the city famous for the catastrophe that took place in the ancient world in 17 AD, during which Pompeii was destroyed by Mother Earth's fury.

Asma Pumpi Moore
BA (Philosophy), LL.B (Hons) UK

CHAPTER ONE

THE EARLY TRAINING CAMP

I WAS NINE YEARS OLD and the summer holidays had just begun. It was about two o'clock in the afternoon. The weather was as hot as ever in Karachi, the temperature having reached 102°F. Humidity made clothes stick to people's skin, but nothing could deter the battalion of eleven boys and one girl, aged between seven and twelve years, from playing hide and seek. The ground was full of empty bottles, trees, and some old, gigantic water pipes, which had been abandoned for years. I was hiding behind the massive leaves of a beautiful palm tree, trying desperately not to be caught, but the thrill and excitement I felt turned to ashes when I heard my mother's voice.

"Pumpi! Where the hell are you?" shouted Mother. Her voice was coming from our house, about fifty yards away from the spot where we were playing. The heat of that anger was enough to boil a thousand kettles. Her tone was enough to warn me that I had to perform some task, which "all good Muslim girls are supposed to do". I ran toward my home, and upstairs to the bedroom where the voice was coming from. As I entered, I saw my mother standing in the main children's bedroom with my eldest brother, Nadir. She gave me a dirty look, as usual. Then she threw something in my face.

"Iron this pair of trousers for Nadir," she demanded.

"What?" I said with repulsion.

What if?

She raised her voice to its highest possible peak.

"Iron Nadir's trousers. Have you lost your hearing?" she repeated her demand.

I couldn't understand why I had to iron his clothes as I was only nine years old. I had never touched an iron, besides we had servants to wash and iron our clothes.

"Why should I iron his clothes? Besides what's happened to Chotta?" (The boy who did the cleaning and ironing), I inquired.

"Servants won't go with you to your husband's house when you get married. You have to learn all these things at an early age. I could even cook when I was your age," she replied angrily.

"Man has gone to the moon; you are still talking about the dark ages," I said in my defence. Mother gritted her teeth. Then she walked toward me, and kneeled down to my height. I was scared, as I could smell her breath on my face. "You are... absolutely right! Man has gone to the moon ... BUT NOT WOMAN! Woman's place is on earth. You better try and keep your feet on the ground! Understand?" Mother explained to me with bitterness.

She pushed me away, and looked into my face with utter hatred. I was desperate to go and join my friends and continue the game.

"I was in the middle of playing hide and seek. I couldn't stop for anything," I replied in anger. I turned around to go back downstairs, but suddenly someone grabbed me from behind! *Tsch*! My mother slapped me across the face, left right, right left.

"Don't try to act like a boy! You are a girl and you will act like a girl! Girls are supposed to listen and obey! If I ask you to do something, you do it," she shouted.

By then, I was immune to her beatings so it didn't bother me. But the fact that I had to do something just because I was born a girl really bothered me.

"I will not do that," I simply said to Mother. She did not like my repudiation.

"Why can't my brother iron his own trousers? After all, he is six years older than me?" I continued. She got up and grabbed me by my hair, and slapped me much harder than the last time. *Tsch…*

"You should iron his trousers because he is your brother," she replied. "You should learn how to serve your brother today, that will enable you to serve your husband tomorrow, You must not forget that God created woman from Adam's rib! What does that teach you?" Mother asked a leading question, quivering with outrage.

" You mean woman was born out of man? Well, then how come men do not produce children? Or at least girls? See it wasn't true". I replied with innocence and sheer confidence.

Mother's face was getting angry, I could see she was squeezing her eyes while starring at my face.

" It was not man's choice to make woman weaker, men did not make women weaker. It was God's decision to make woman weaker to test her obedience towards God" Mother explained. Anger flowed through my veins. I was made to feel that being a girl was to be a lower class citizen.

I ran to my bedroom and came back with one of my *shalwar* (trousers), and asked my mother to ask my brother to iron my *shalwar* first. My mother was enraged to see my attitude and hostility toward basic Islamic traditions. I could feel her eyes piercing my face, and her anger stabbing at my ribs. I was wounded although I wasn't bleeding. She pulled my hair, grabbed me and slapped me across the face several times. Then she hit me with her slipper. Her violence did not stop there; she got hold of a massive dictionary, and then came a BANG! She hit me with that thick tome.

"Try to act like a Muslim girl, shame on you! You are Syed's daughter, and if you don't behave properly, people won't respect you," she shouted at the top of her voice. My head hurt from her pulling my hair, and the blow from the book. By that time, one of our neighbours, Mrs Kabeer, came upstairs. Unfortunately, it's obligatory in our culture to interfere in other people's business.

Asian philosophy is "My business is to interfere with everybody's business and everybody's business is to interfere in my business!"

For a second I thought she might rescue me. But my mother told her about my audacious attitude. Mrs Kabeer felt outrage towards me.

"How come you can't control such a little girl? People tame their lions; you can't control a nine-year-old child! What kind of a mother are you? If she were my daughter, I would have crushed her like an ant by now. She has an evil spirit in her," Mrs Kabeer challenged Mother.

However, she was a woman who prayed to Allah five times a day, while behind their backs she character-assassinated every woman and her daughters. Although backbiting is a sin in Islam, she considered herself as one of the decent Muslims on Campus. Her constant verbal encouragement intensified my mother's rage. She took a metal hanger out of the cupboard and hit me repeatedly. I was devastated and humiliated. I not only had a dictator, but a spectator as well.

The strikes on my bare legs and feet were awful. I wanted to cover my legs with my tiny hands, but the blows hurt my hands. I screamed and begged my mother to stop, but she did not. All of a sudden my brother got hold of the hanger and stopped my mother.

"I think she got the message," he said to her. I got up, but started to limp as my legs hurt severely. I saw blood oozing from my hands and legs, as my skin had been torn apart: along with my heart. All through my childhood, I had a strong feeling that I was not my mother's child. The feeling of being a motherless child was spreading like cancer; slowly but surely, eating me alive. She and her friend, Mrs Kabeer, then left the room.

Mother's attitude seemed eccentric to me. Perhaps that's what she thought about mine. I believe the feeling was mutual!

I felt bad for myself, but worse about their orthodox thinking. I knew I would never want to have respect from egocentric Muslim men, because their opinion had no meaning in my life. Whether they thought I was as pious as Mother Teresa, or a low-class tart, their opinion never mattered to me.

My whole body felt stiff. My legs were killing me. I looked down at my knees, and saw blood pouring from my legs. My tiny hands and forearms were bleeding as well, as I had tried to hide my face when that cruel woman was bashing me. The metal hanger had slashed my skin. I sat on the floor, hid my face with my hands, and wept bitterly.

I didn't know what I was crying for. Was it because of a sense of lack of love, or lack of understanding from my mother, or perhaps both? One thing was for sure; I was not crying about the fact that I was a girl! I went to the bathroom to wash my legs and arms. I then put on some toothpaste, as I couldn't think of any other way to stop the blood flow. I was quite happy to find out that it did stop the blood. But there was no remedy for my internal wounds.

In Pakistan there was no institute like the NSPCC. I came back into the bedroom and looked outside the window where all the boys were still playing hide and seek. Their mothers would never call them to do domestic chores because they were boys. Asian boys are the kings of their kingdom.

In Pakistan, as in many Muslim countries, Muslim men, fathers, brothers and husbands, run the lives and determine the destiny of young Muslim women, in the name of Islam. But it is a great tragedy that women, as mothers, also play a major part in suppressing the voices of women, daughters and sisters, in order to please their husbands.

Every time I raised an issue about prejudice against women, my mother would try to shut my mouth. It was one of those days when she grasped hold of my throat.

"If you give me another lecture about girls and their rights, and what they should and should not do, I will cut your tongue out!" she said. Then she pushed me away. I was disgusted by the threat. I started to cry. My anger was boiling inside me, and I had no way to let it out. It was like a volcano waiting to erupt! I could not control myself; despite the beating, I stood in front of her, tears streaming down my face.

"I know and I know that you know that it is not right that girls should be treated so badly" I said. Before I had even finished my sentence, my mother ran to the other room. She came back with a pair of scissors, and grabbed me by the throat again. She lay my neck on her lap, and put pressure on my throat.

"Open your mouth! Open your mouth! I am going to cut your tongue out today!" She was screaming her head off. I knew all that drama was to show my father that she was a mother who could control her daughter, and to teach my younger sisters a lesson. I clenched my teeth tightly. At the age of nine, I was mortified; my heart was tumbling. I believed my mother was going to cut out my tongue. My terror was at its peak. I felt helpless in a world full of grownups! I still remember the terror on my younger sisters' faces. They stood there rigid. My head was tilted, and my mother held my face sideways.

"Open your mouth," she demanded violently.

She then asked my brother to help her open my mouth.

"I have to go to Raza's house." I felt relieved when he replied that he had to go to his friend's house. He then gave me a sad look and left.

Those three or four minutes of torture are unforgettable, as well as unforgivable! Hence I could see the purpose of that exercise was to teach my younger sisters: "Do not follow Pumpi's steps, but be a puppet". My sisters were crying hysterically. They asked Mother for forgiveness. I felt the grip of my mother's hand on my throat loosen, and then suddenly she pushed me away. While I lay on the floor, she kicked me in the stomach. I felt as if I was naked. It was as if somebody had stripped me of my dignity. However, my lack of remorse prevented me from asking for her forgiveness.

In an Asian Islamic culture the status of a mother is like the Pope in the Vatican!

One should not question his word, or his virtue. He is the absolute truth.

A mother can never do wrong! All through my childhood in Pakistan, I had nowhere to go to complain about her outrageous behaviour, but the bitter fact is that even after all those years, when people read my story, they will still condemn me for pointing the finger at my mother. However, these mothers should know they are being used by men as the messengers of male domination.

Even as a little child, seeing that grown-up women were the object of prejudice was painful for me. But being a boy is like being one of those old Indian Maharajas! Where servants surround you.

It was hard for me to comprehend the contradictory ideology of Islamic teaching. The Koran says everybody is equal, yet in reality women have no authority to do anything. As a daughter, she is the responsibility of her father. As a wife, her husband.

As a little girl, all I saw was younger and older sisters serving their brothers like kings. One of my friends, Sadia, had five sisters and two brothers. The moment their oldest brother Asif, came home, they were like maids to him. One of them took off his shoes; the other brought him water. Although I was only ten years old at the time, seeing that made me feel sick. I asked her older brother, who was enjoying the pampering, whether he was unwell. He replied, "No." Then I asked him why he couldn't do things for himself. Asif didn't like the manner in which I asked the question, nor the question itself. He told me the same old Islamic maxim that women were made to serve men, while men were made to look after them.

I was furious at his remark. I took my friend, Sadia, his sister, aside and told her it couldn't be true. I still remember Sadia's face dropping.

"Pumpi, I think you are losing your mind. You are mad. I don't want to go to hell, therefore I will do what is going to take me to heaven," Sadia said.

I was shocked, as I had always believed Sadia was a very smart girl. I was disappointed by her reply.

The most disturbing factor for me was that we were living on a University Campus, where people were highly educated. Nevertheless, they did not allow their minds to be open to their maximum capacity. It was a very painful thing for me to understand that these intelligent women had accepted the norms of these insidious traditions, in the name of Islam.

Were these rules made by men to overpower women? Are men frightened to see the strength of women, and therefore suppress them? Or have I misunderstood the Holy book?

What if?

In our Asian culture, which is based on man-made Muslim values, girls are supposed to be quiet and pretend they don't have a voice. But they have to make sure that they have ears to listen! The attitude of mothers toward their little girls is barbaric. Islamic society expects mothers to train their daughters to be good, obedient wives. As most children spend a lot of time with their mothers, the task of parenthood is their sole responsibility. On closer examination, we see that these women are given the highest status as mothers and teachers. The respect women receive cloaks men's ulterior motives, which is the feeding of male dominance to the young brains.

In a way, an Asian Muslim household is set up like an army regime; Father is the general whom you never saw. However, his loyal corporal (his wife) carries out his orders. That's what my mother was doing. I was the first daughter; therefore, it was imperative for my mother to make sure I unquestioningly followed the path that had been followed by women for centuries; this would enable my sisters to follow the right Muslim way.

Was I alone?

The next day I told my friends what my mother had asked me to do. I was shocked to hear that all six of my friends had been washing their brother's jeans, ironing their clothes, and cleaning their rooms for two years, despite the fact they all had servants. I asked them why.

"I have to learn how to look after my husband when I grow up. Mum told me that every girl should know how to cook, clean and wash, but washing jeans by hand is really hard work," they replied calmly.

I was ashamed of my friends. I almost felt they had disgraced me! One of the girls who was nine years old, and whose brother was only five years old, got less pocket money than him because she was a girl! At the same time, I felt deeply sorry for them. The other friends were of the same opinion that we should look after the brothers, i.e. serve them. I told them 'no way', we are not their slaves; we should be treated like boys. My inner desire for equal treatment got me into trouble. A few of my friends then refused to do the washing for their brothers, and asked their brothers to do their ironing themselves. I ended up being the person that exploited their tender minds. Although I was the same age! Some mothers refused to let their daughters play with me, as I was thought to have an 'evil spirit'.

SUMMER HOLIDAYS

I was about eleven years old by this time. We were visiting one of my father's friends in Lahore. It was our summer holidays. Due to my passion for drawing and painting, I took my sketch board and pencils with me. It was about 8pm, and I was busy sketching, when I noticed a man of about twenty-five years old staring at my sketches. He was the son of my father's friend. His name was Tariq, and he was a student at the Lahore Fine Art College. He was absolutely astonished at my drawings. It was the first time anybody had said anything positive about my life. Tariq took the sketchbook to Lahore Fine Art College without telling me, to show it to his teachers.

Next day at the dining table, Tariq told all of us that he had shown my drawings to his teachers in the Art College and they thought Pumpi had a rare talent. Suddenly at the tender age of eleven I felt I was being given a chance to graduate in Art. I was thrilled! But my parents had to consider the customs of the time, and could not allow "a girl" to live away from her parents. I begged them to let me go and learn art. My parents were shocked that I could even imagine asking them such a question. I was a Muslim girl, who was the responsibility of 'the father'! I was not supposed to look after or make choices for myself. I felt defeated by the Islamic norms once again. I was beginning to think that Islam was my biggest enemy, but then I realized that the real enemy was Muslim men. These people were like germs, which gives the disease a bad name.

During my time in Pakistan, I felt trapped in the manmade culture. It was devastating to see women forced to act as men's slaves. I felt deeply for them, but as a freethinking person now, it is more devastating to know that these women don't even acknowledge the fact that they are in prison, and that they DO have rights! They have been hypnotized by men to believe that they are inferior to men.

LET ME IN

August 27th. I was rushing to get ready to see my friend, Rubina, as it was her birthday party. I put on my pink frock and white socks, and quickly glanced in the mirror, but was shocked to see someone else in the mirror! My mother was standing behind me. She said, "Why are you wearing a frock? Didn't I tell you that you should cover your legs? In Islam women's legs should be covered."

I said, "I don't care. I love this frock, and I can't wear a bloody *shalwar*. In any case I hate wearing *shalwars*, plus why would God give us legs if we have to hide them?"

Mother simply pulled my hair, and pulled my face toward her. She clenched her teeth and slapped me across the face. "You are getting out of hand. I am getting complaints from other mothers that you are teaching their daughters to be as wild as you are. Pumpi, nobody will like you if you disrespect your parents and make fun of your religion."

I pulled myself away from her and said, " I don't care. I think the whole system stinks like a rotten egg! Everything is against girls and in favour of boys. Did you ever stop Nadir or Peecho from doing anything?"

Her reply was the same old one, "Boys can do whatever they want! *Zamana* (Society) will spit on you if you put a foot wrong!" She made her statement in a loud voice and left the room.

I was told quite clearly that girls are of less value: however I never felt ashamed of being a girl! It never caused my beliefs to falter. I pitied people who felt that girls were of less value in Islamic Society.

Because of my conflict with my mother or other women in the neighbourhood about the treatment of girls, I knew one of us had to be wrong here! Was it me, a seven-year-old child or a 1400-year-old Islamic tradition? Surely a system that had been in place for centuries couldn't be wrong? Thousands of young girls had been through what was in effect 'slavery'. They merely lived and died, but never questioned the system. They were never allowed to doubt the system. By casting doubt upon the way things were, they would have been able to seek knowledge! Were they right not to question, or were they not able to question? Maybe they knew they would never be able to get the answers?

As I walked to my friend Rubina's eighth birthday party, a flood of questions followed me. I ignored them and kept on walking, holding onto the present, which I had wrapped the night before. It was a beautiful doll, and I knew Rubina would love it. As I could hear my friends shouting and playing, I began to run faster. My heart was pounding with joy. Rubina's house was only forty yards away from our house.

Unfortunately, upon my arrival at her house, I saw her mother standing on the doorstep like a bouncer at a nightclub! My heart plunged as I saw the anger in her face. The heat from her eyes melted my joy. The excitement and thrill turned into confusion and ambiguity. I could see that she had something on her mind. I knew I was in trouble again, but what for?

"Where the hell do you think you are going, you evil girl?" she asked with a smirk on her face.

"It's Rubina's birthday today! She did invite me. In fact I was the first one to be given the invitation because I'm her 'best friend'," I replied with utmost pride and joy. I handed her the present hoping she would let me inside.

Instead, she handed me a small notebook with my handwriting. It read:

GIRLS = BOYS CLUB

Head: Pumpi Hameed.

Secretary: Rubina Ansar.

Rules:

Ask 4 equal pocket money as your brothers.

Go alone if the brother can go alone.

If u wash the jeans of your brother: make sure he washes your shalwars.
Wear frock n socks if u like.

I felt I was caught red-handed. I was tremendously nervous and terrified to see that our secret club diary had been revealed! I was petrified. I started to twist my fingers, and bit my lips. She turned to the next page, which had MEMBERS NAMES; thirteen girls' names were there. I was frightened. The thought that if my mother saw this I would definitely be beaten to death this time, flashed through my mind.

I was horrified, but was also desperate to join the birthday party. I could hear the other children singing Ring-a-ring-a-roses. I tried to squeeze through the gap in the door, but Rubina's mother put her foot on the door. Then she put her hand towards me and pushed me back, stopping me from getting in. I felt very low and deeply shocked. I was being treated like an evil girl whose only crime was to express what she felt justifiable at the time. Ironically, after thirty years, she still feels the same injustice in the same country. But at that young age, I was unaware of the fact that this was a country where women are supposed to act like a flock of sheep! If one goes to one side: the rest must follow. Regardless of the fact that the first sheep may be heading toward the edge of a cliff!

"You are an evil girl. How come you are born into Syed's family? You are a disgrace to your descendent. You are trying to exploit these nice Muslim girls: get out of here," ordered Rubina's mother without hesitation.

I was numbed, but indignant. The stream of tears

poured down my face. At the age of eight, if you are expelled from your friend's birthday party, you feel you are at the edge of a cliff, about to fall, and everybody is watching and waiting for you to fall, so they can laugh at you! The world seems to crumble onto your tiny shoulders. I was devastated. The time stood still for me. I had waited all day for 5pm, for her birthday party. My throat was dry, and my face was wet with tears.

"Aunt, I am sorry! Please let me go to the party." I plucked up the courage and begged her. It felt like somebody was squeezing my heart.

Again I tried to move towards the open door where she was standing. But this time, she grabbed my small hand.

"It is about time that you learnt your lesson! Your mother told me you have an evil spirit. Even Mrs Kabeer told me you have no respect for Muslim rules. You should get this into your mind: girls have to listen to fathers, brothers, and finally to their husbands. Evil girls like you have no place in our society," she explained, pointing at the gate.

Out! Out, Pumpi. I don't want Rubina to listen to your evil thoughts," she said with authority. I cried and held both hands together, pleading with her.

"Please! Let me play," I begged. I will never forget the triumphant look of glory on her face. I was desperate to win the losing battle. I stood there and kept asking her again and again. I had no choice but to walk back to my home, which was five minutes away, knowing my brothers and sisters would make fun of me for being expelled from the party.

A cloud of humiliation hovered over me. I vividly

remember walking back. My feet felt heavy, as if I was not walking over earth, but the earth was walking over me. I held Rubina's present close to my heart, my tears making it wet. I knew that my best friend would be missing me. I decided to go back to her house, so that I could at least leave the present at the door. As a child "the birthday present" was the most important thing. I walked back slowly and sadly. This time the door was closed. I took a deep sigh and knelt down. I then placed the present at the foot of the door, although it felt more as if I were putting a wreath on a grave. My heart wept and tears rolled down my cheeks. I walked away from the door, but could not leave the pain behind. I missed the birthday party from which I was banned! I thought of climbing a tree where I could have a full view of the birthday party. I could see girls in multi-coloured frocks running around like crazy. "HAPPY BIRTHDAY TO YOU," they shouted. I burst into a raging sea of tears. I felt somebody had put chains around me. I had strength and courage, but the more I tried to break the chains, the tighter they became.

Needless to say, Rubina's mother stopped her playing with me. But Rubina and I were like two bodies in one soul. We decided a 'code'. And the code was the street pole. The idea was that if Rubina wanted to play with me she would come out and hit the pole with a stone three times, which would alert me that Rubina was waiting for me. We managed to keep our innocent friendship alive in this secret manner for many years.

Then one day I insisted on having my hair cut as short as my brother's, something my mother would not allow. In

Islam, when a woman dies her hair should be long enough to cover her breasts. Any woman whose breast is not covered by her hair would be thrown into hell. That was the lame excuse I was given by local female scholars. In my little mind I used to think who cares once you are dead whether your hair covers your breast or pussy? Any way, that is one of the reason Muslim women have long hair. As Mother often used to leave us at the hairdresser's while doing her shopping. I nagged the hairdresser to cut my hair as short as boys. And eventually got the 'boy cut hair style' (as they say in Pakistan). Mother was furious to see my face. Her verbal abuse was a daily dose for me, therefore I couldn't care less.

It was just after this hair cut that Rubina and I were at Yasmin's house. (Yasmin was another mutual friend). Yasmin was much older than either of us. And her family was more orthodox than ours. Yasmin's family was outraged to see my hair. They started to condemn my parents and call them *Kafir* (non-believers of God). They told me that in Islam women's hair should be long, and on the day of judgement, women's breasts are supposed to be covered with their hair. And any woman whose breasts are not covered would be thrown into hell. I did not accept that philosophy and started to argue (as usual).

When Yasmin's father and mother left Yasmin's room, I was furious and aggressive. I took the scissors out from Yasmin's dressing table and in no time grabbed her and cut her long hair into 'uneven short hair'. Because Yasmin was struggling, her hair was an absolute mess. Rubina started to laugh at my wildness, however, Yasmin's cries brought her parents and uncle to the room. As soon as I saw them I ran like a cheetah! By now it was six o'clock in the evening: most of the parents were outside their homes having a chat with their neighbours (in a typically Asian way) and there was Mr Hameed's daughter, aged thirteen, being chased by Yasmin's father, two male cousins and her uncle! It was another blow to my parents' respectable name. I was thin like a needle, I was running very fast, but did not know where I was going The only good thing was the area we were living in Karachi was extremely safe. After a long time I noticed there was no sound of steps. I realized that I had left them far behind. I found myself far away from the house. I knew the reason for my anger was because Yasmin's parents were saying bad things about my parents. But what was strange at that time was for me to feel for my parents.

Although I was crying and justifying my action of cutting poor Yasmin's hair, sitting on this broken wall of an old school, I knew my brothers and parents were going to beat me up really badly this time. I thought I could live in that broken building for a few weeks until they cooled down. I was frightened to death: cutting someone's daughter's hair out of rage was not a decent thing at all, by any standard, and, especially in a strict Muslim household like Yasmin's; it was not a petty crime. I thought I could stay the night there, as my parents would never know in a big house whether I was there or not. The night was falling. The noise of mosquitoes was terrible. The heat was unbearable. I was extremely dehydrated. Suddenly I heard some men talking outside the building. I froze as I recognized the voices of my eldest brother and two servants. Before they entered the broken building, I ran out of the other side, I managed to slip through quietly. In our house the back door is normally open till everybody has gone to sleep. I ran like a mad dog. It was a very hard to see exactly where I was, before I could head for home. I had no idea of time. I felt it was really late as all the *chokidars* (petrol men) were out and they usually come out after 10pm. I did not want to ask them as every body knows everybody in our culture, whether you live in the UK or Karachi University. Eventually I saw the small white houses, I knew those were D block, and we were in C block. I had no strength to run, and I had no reason to run as nobody was chasing me: they were looking for me. I eventually found the house. The back door was ajar. I peeked in with pumping heart and frightened soul. I ran to the downstairs toilet and locked myself in. I did not switch on the light as I knew my parents might find out that somebody was in the toilet. I did not even know whether they were awake or asleep. Now being a mother, it seems such a stupid question to even think that parents could be asleep, the night their daughter had disappeared!

In the toilet I drank as much water as I possibly could. I was waiting for the right moment to run upstairs to my bedroom, when I heard someone trying to open the toilet door. I looked at the small window where the moonlight was showing. At first I thought I should climb out and let the person use the toilet and then sneak back in. Before I finalized my thoughts, there was someone outside pushing the doors violently.

A voice said, "Pumpi, I know it's you." It was my brother, Billo, because he had been my secret keeper all my teens, I quickly opened the door. I still remember the glow on his face and his scream, "*Ammi* (mother) she is alive, she is fine." My mother and father came running toward me. I saw my mother's nose was red as she had been crying. One by one all the seven brothers, sisters and two servants were there. I was shocked, why was nobody hitting me? Then my younger sister came forward and bust into tears and said, "We thought some truck driver had taken you away. We thought we would never see you again." My father and mother went back to the living room to call relatives to inform them about my safe return. I was shocked to see everybody so upset, as I was expecting anger, not tears, on my return. I walked to the living room and noticed the time it was 4:50 in the morning. I was starving, the poor servant made chapattis and brought them for me. I did not know at that time that they had been looking for me all evening and all my family members were so concerned. As a teenager I was blind to the concern of the family members. I missed school the next day and slept in. But in the evening both of my parents came to my room and did what I was expecting them to do. Their verbal abuse was too painful, but I suppose I deserved it for hiding in the school all evening; as far as hair chopping was concerned, I had no regrets.

In my opinion women have no significant role or respect in an Asian society. Women are treated as machinery, which can be operated by men. Their sole role is to produce children and chapattis in abundance. The only respect they command is as a 'mother'. And even that role is only given to women because men have an ulterior motive. Men know that children's formative years are spent with their mothers, and by giving mothers this role they leave the ultimate power in the women's hands. However, these women are answerable to their husbands. And you are not a good wife if your daughters are not obeying men – men as brothers, fathers, and ultimately husbands. The status of a mother is unquestionable. Therefore children who are physically and mentally abused by their mothers have no way of complaining; they have to live in the prison into which they have been born.

Our house was no different from most other Muslim households in Pakistan. Where sons are given the ultimate freedom and daughters are told what to do! It is a society where people fear other people's opinion. That fear overrides the fear of God. In the name of Islam, girls are to cover their legs, arms, even their faces: while boys can go outside and play in shorts!

In the normal Muslim Asian household, father is the ruler. Girls only do what he allows them to do. Young women have to live under their father's or husband's shadow all their lives. Young boys can go and live abroad, while young girls are not even allowed to go to the local shops alone. Growing up, I remember that whenever I asked for something, I was told that *Abbu* (Father) allowed it or didn't allow it! I questioned my mother one day, "I am thirteen years old. Why can't I wear what I want to wear? Why can't I put on lipstick? Why can't I wear makeup?"

"While daughters are under their father's protection

they have to do what they are told, not what they want," Mother said.

"Would I be allowed to wear a sleeveless blouse and sari once I am married?" I asked. "Only if your husband allowed you to do so! You have to understand that daughters are their father's responsibility before the marriage, and after the marriage they are their husband's responsibility," Mother replied. I felt like an object, not a human being. I was outraged.

"If you want to make God happy you have to make your parents happy, by listening to them. You must not forget that you are Syed's daughter. You must obey Islamic laws. And once you are married, you have to make sure your husband is happy with you if you want to go to heaven!" she added.

"We, as women, don't really live! We are like animals that are sold for slaughter, not even like pets! People don't give away their pets! But as girls we have one owner till we are mature, then we are sold, without cash, to another buyer who can afford to feed us," I retorted.

My sisters started to laugh at me, while my mother was furious. She snatched my little radio from my hand as punishment for speaking my mind.

The curse of God?

One day when I was thirteen years old, I felt very tired all day at school, but I wasn't sure why. As soon as my school bus approached my house I felt relieved. I ran to the toilet, and was shocked to see that my shalwar was full of blood! I felt terrified. I had never seen blood on anybody's clothes before. I didn't know what to do, and worse, what had I done to cause this? My first thought was that Mother would kill me! I couldn't go out, as somebody would see the stains on my shalwar.

Then I checked my dress, and to my horror the stains had leaked onto the whole school uniform. Mother was going to beat me up again.

I was shocked and horrified, and wondered what I had done to cause such bleeding. I was petrified. I was the eldest girl, and had no one other than my mother to tell me what had happened. I called my younger sister, and asked her to call Mother. I was crying bitterly because of the shock. My sister called my mother three times, and told her that Pumpi was in the toilet crying hysterically, but she took no notice.

Then through the window, I saw my eldest brother passing by. I told him that something had happened, and my *shalwar* (trousers) were covered in blood. He was much older than me, and I suppose he knew what was happening. He ran and called Mother. She came to the toilet, and instead of consoling me shouted, "I told you not to ride bicycles and climb trees like boys. Now look what you've done." Then she gave me a pad, and told me to put it into my panties.

"*Ammi*, what happened to me? Am I going to die?" I asked through my tears.

"I don't know. How should I know? You jump and run like boys. I told you to behave like a girl, now see what has happened," she replied without any concern whatsoever.

"How long does it take to stop? Will I die?" I asked again. I kept crying and my whole body was shaking with terror.

As a teenager, it was hard to comprehend living, never mind dying!

I was petrified, as death seemed to be very close to me. The fear of dying is worse than death itself. I rubbed my hands together, as they were extremely cold. I looked at Mother with pleading eyes to save me.

"See! This is the curse of God on you. Well, now ask God to forgive you for your sharp tongue. And promise never to speak evil against Islam," she told me. I was mortified.

Whether I would die or survive was the question that was making me panicky. In Pakistan, there is no concept of 'sex education' in schools. The word 'sex' itself is forbidden. I had never seen nor heard that blood could pour from the private parts of your body. Therefore, for me it was terrible.

Night fell, and I lay on my bed, although it was as if I were lying in a coffin. I wasn't sure whether or not I would still be alive in the morning. My pillow was soaked with tears. I remember vividly how loudly in my heart I cried for God to forgive me. I urged him to stop my bleeding, because it horrified me. I put the cotton pad into my panties every half an hour. But I kept checking the bleeding every fifteen minutes to see whether or not it had stopped. The bleeding did not stop until morning. Each hour my terror increased. I closed my bedroom door, sat on the floor, and begged God to forgive me for my sins, and stop my bleeding. I begged Him not to let any of my friends know that he had cursed me. I don't know how long I cried and prayed at the same time.

A few days later I noticed that the bleeding had stopped. I took out my brother's bicycle, and started to climb trees again. But then, a few weeks later, the same thing happened, and by that time I was sure God was cross with me! I slowed down my running around and became a very quiet and sad girl. I carried the heavy burden of guilt on my tender shoulders, because my mother led me to believe I had done something drastically wrong, and that it was is my retribution time. It was Sunday afternoon, and I was at my friend Nasreen's house, which was twenty yards away from our house. Nasreen was a few years older than me. She and I were playing with magic cards when she told me she needed to go to the toilet. As she turned around, I saw a big bloodstain on her green dress. I was shocked and saddened at the same time to see that God had cursed her too! By that time, Nasreen had left the room, and I was alone with my thoughts. Soon after, she came back, got something from the cupboard, and ran back to the toilet.

"Nasreen, you had a blood stain on your dress," I said to her, when she finally came back. She laughed and ran to the toilet again, and changed her favourite green dress. When she came back this time, she was still smiling at me. Perhaps she could not read the confusion on my face.

"How come you aren't upset?" I asked her.

"Upset about what?" she asked calmly.

"That God is punishing you for your sins. You are bleeding, aren't you?" I explained.

Nasreen's laughter filled the room.

"Pumpi, who told you that it is a punishment for your sins? *Pagul* (crazy), every woman has to go through this. It is a natural female cycle. It has nothing to do with being bad or good as a person," she said disbelievingly.

I was highly confused by her ambiguous reply. Nasreen's laughter was still in the room, but I was not sure what she was laughing at. Was that my innocence or madness? Nasreen then explained to me in detail that it was called "menstruation". I told her that for the past few months I had been constantly praying to God to stop this. She started to laugh again, and then took me to her eldest sister, Anjum. Anjum was very sympathetic towards me. I told her how my cruel mother had made me believe for months that I had done something wrong.

I felt ecstatic to know that it was not my fault. It had nothing to do with riding a bike or climbing trees as Mother had accused me. The whole incident was very traumatic to comprehend. I remember trying very hard that night, while sobbing into my pillow, to understand why she hated me so much.

The next morning I wanted to ask her why she had lied to me. But the look of venom and wave of hatred coming from her eyes made me change my mind.

Every month when I asked her to buy me sanitary towels, I had to go through a period of humiliation before she gave them to me. She made me feel as if I had committed a crime, for which she had to pay the price.

Then the point came when I could no longer ask her for sanitary towels. I would steal them from her bathroom, or from neighbour's houses, when I used their toilets. For the sheer humiliation that woman, who was supposed to be my mother, put me through, only God can forgive; a human heart is not kind enough. Once I didn't have a chance to steal any sanitary towels, and had to use a cloth instead. I was extremely embarrassed when, in the school playground, it fell out. I wanted the earth to open, and swallow me up. I could see some girls laughing loudly at me, while others tried hard to contain their laughter. I was crying with embarrassment. My screams were louder than the roar of a lion. My tears ran into my mouth.

I saw Miss Halima, my teacher, walking toward me. She came close to me, and asked all the girls to go to the other playground. She then put her arms around me and asked me what had happened. After listening to my plight, she touched my shoulder.

"Don't worry, daughter, it will be all right," she said gently. I then walked with her to the staff room, where she told me about the first time she got her period. She made me feel very proud to be a woman. She told me she would call my mother, and things would get better. After that, I got sanitary towels regularly from her, without even asking.

Privacy is a luxury

One of the best and worst features of Asian or Muslim society is its closeness. That means everyone's business is everyone else's; privacy is a luxury. This is a close-knit society – but with the negative characteristic of being oppressive and overly judgmental.

"Freedom is the oxygen of the Soul!" – Moshe Dayan

It was late afternoon during the hot summer of Karachi. My whole family was fast asleep, including the servants, which gave me the ideal opportunity to fly my brother's kite for several hours. I was only seven years old, and thoroughly enjoying flying a kite. The strong wind made my pink frock fly toward my face. I was trying to push the frock down, and at the same time keep a grip on the thread of the kite in my hand. My joy was at its peak, when I saw my neighbour's son, who was quite a lot older than me, coming towards me on the huge playing field. The anger on his face was obvious. He then said, "Pumpi, have you gone mad? Boys play with kites, not girls."

He then grabbed me by the arm, and brought me back to my parents' house. As I was reaching my home, I saw two women, who came towards me and said, "Shame on you, you are a disgrace to Muslim girls."

At that moment my mind ceased to comprehend: what was so awful about flying a kite? The young man knocked at the door, woke up my parents, and told them what I had been doing. Considering his excessive anger, one would imagine I had been attempting to kill somebody! My mother was obviously distressed that her daughter was so out of control that a young man had to bring her home.

"Why can't you understand that you are a girl?" she started to yell at me. "Girls have to keep themselves intact. If you lose your respect in the eyes of society, you will have no place to live," Mother warned me.

"What's wrong with flying a kite? Why can't I do what boys do?" I questioned her.

"Because you are a G-I-R-L! In the Koran, God asked girls to be in the house and boys to go out. A girl's place is in the 'house' not in the playground. In Islam, girls are supposed to cover their legs, not like you with your frock flying around, and playing with the kite, just like K said. What a great shame. You are the daughter of a Syed," Mother screamed at me.

At that time I felt that I was a guilty person, and that my crime was being born a girl. I was extremely distressed and frustrated at this stage. The young, tender mind of this little girl could not accept the fact that, on one hand, God could be so logical as to say that whatever we do we must pay the price for our bad actions; yet on the other hand, could God be so stupid as to ask little girls to hide their tiny legs? What harm could they possibly inflict? Why on earth would God, the source of knowledge, ask one human being to serve another human being? It did not make sense.

I felt a burning desire inside me to shake society. It was like a full term foetus ready for the 'birth'!

Jungle of bewilderment

In most Islamic Societies, a father decides a woman's destiny. Therefore, the girl has to spend the rest of her life with a man whom she had probably never seen before. Yet she is supposed to 'serve' him to the best of her capabilities. This biased and bizarre system is called an Arranged Marriage, based on Islamic values as follows:

The Holy Koran; sorah An-Nisa; (The Woman) 1V

34: Men are the protectors and maintainers of women, because Allah has made one of them to excel the other, and because they spend (to support them) from their means.

In light of this, girls are supposed to be looked after by the male members of the family. A daughter is a father's responsibility, a sister is a brother's responsibility, and a wife is a husband's responsibility. These statements have made men the creator of women's destinies in most Muslim countries, and Pakistan is no different.

Growing up in Karachi, I could see that most Islamic

rules were carefully carved out to suit men, and give them the maximum liberty, while at the same time depriving women of the right to exercise their free will. However, can the human mind accept that God, the source of justice, could be ruthlessly unfair to women?

Pakistan is an Islamic country, and as in any Islamic country, girls have no say in most of life's major decisions. From an early age they are told what to do, either by their mothers, younger brothers, or fathers. This concept of having to obey others, and not being allowed to express their own views has led them to believe their opinion was somehow inferior. In reality, women are treated like slaves in most Islamic countries. The only difference is that they do not have visible shackles around their feet. Throughout my childhood I could never accept the fact put to me that women should be submissive to men; therefore men have been given power over women. I had the audacity to ask scholars and my parents to give me some kind of validation that the words they were quoting came from God.

As a little girl I still remember the amount of time I spent writing to God, asking Him all the questions that were confusing my well-being, and questioning my sole existence, and then running to post those letters. My brothers and sisters would laugh at me. For three brothers and three sisters all Islamic teachings were an absolute guide for decent living. One by one, all my brothers and sisters finished reading the Koran. But every time my parents hired a *Mulla* for me, I demanded to read in Urdu (my native tongue) so I could understand what I was reading. However, for some bizarre reason it was accepted that you could only read the translation once you had read the entire Koran in Arabic. I always managed to read the translation first; therefore, by the time the *Mulla* came, I would throw several questions about the Koran at him. Therefore in the eyes of most *Mullas* I was seen as the *Shetan* (devil).

At one stage no *Mulla* was prepared to come to our house to teach Pumpi the Koran. In a culture where every child finishes reading the Koran by the age of nine or ten and I was already fifteen years old and hadn't finished the Holy book, I was seen as a bad-spirited girl. Several times I questioned my religious teachers at school, as well as my parents about the prejudicial voice in our culture. I was told that science needed proof, not religion. Religion is a faith, which should be accepted, as has been taught for many centuries. Every time I raised a question about the Islamic teachings, I was reminded that in the Koran it says that

Mohammed's (peace be unto him) word is the word of God. But how do we know that it is the word of God? The answer was, "Because Mohammed (peace be unto him) said so."

I said, "How do we know that Mohammed (peace be unto him) was the messenger of Allah?"

They said, "The Koran said so."

For me it was like the little boy's explanation when his teacher asked him where he lived.

He said, "In front of the post office."

The teacher said, "Where is the post office?" He replied innocently, "Right in front of my house."

The teacher was getting angry by this stage, and asked

the boy, "Where are both of them?" The child replied with no regrets, "In front of EACH OTHER!"

At the age of seven, it was hard to believe that even grownups could be stupid! But I had to! Although that did not make me a genius, I was still the same confused, stubborn little girl.

But my question was and still is, "How do we know that it is the word of Mohammed (peace be unto him)?" If one believes in the fairness of God, then these teachings are contradictory. If one believes in the Adam and Eve story in the Koran, then it does not make sense why, at one time, brothers and sisters were having sex to multiply the human race, and then the law conveniently changed and it became incest!

THE OPPRESSION AND DEVALUATION OF WOMEN

The Koran contains references to the equality of all believers, male and female, before God. But in practice, the interpretation of Islam is done by the men: for the men. It is very carefully carved to suit men, and give them maximum liberty. Meanwhile, it deprives women of the right to exercise their free will. Men have been given great authority over women in the form of a father, brother, and when she marries, she is under the control of her husband, and must treat him as a god.

Growing up as a child, it was like an unsolved mystery to me. The way one set of human beings were fully covered, yet others (men) walked around bare-chested. My tiny, stubborn mind could not understand this, and was therefore unable to accept the fact that women were weaker than men!

What if?

It was late 1980, and the whole family had been invited to a big dinner party. During dinner, I overheard that one of the women, a lecturer at Karachi University, could not go for '*haaj*' (religious pilgrimage/ God's home) because she was not married. A single woman is NOT allowed to go alone to *haaj*!

I was tormented to hear that. In that room full of educated people, I opened my mouth once again.

"Muslim men have twisted every angle of Islam to make sure that women walk behind them," I said in disgust.

All eyes turned from the dinner table toward me. I felt confident about myself. But the moment I saw my father and mother looking at me, I knew I would pay a very high price if I expressed my viewpoints on this occasion.

"It is not men's word, it is Mohammed's word! (peace be upon him) You are Syed's daughter, you should know that Mohammed's (peace be upon him) word is God's word," one of the lecturers said.

"Who is the source of justice?" I asked her.

She was surprised I had the courage to ask the question.

"Of course, God," she replied.

"Could the source of justice be so unfair in his dealings with his people? There can be only two things; either God is fair or he is not fair!" I continued my challenge. We all do agree that God is fair! And if he is fair, how can he make one set of people superior to others? This very concept itself defeats the ethos of the fairness of God!" I said with utmost confidence.

There was a deep silence, broken only by an unheard voice.

Growing up, as a young Islamic girl, I felt ashamed to be associated with an institution that had discrimination against women in every field.

I wanted to make people aware of the fact that the root of discrimination is fear! Fear leads to threat! God does not need to fear anyone! God is the ultimate source of power! He does not need to feel threatened by anyone! Therefore, God would not discriminate against women!

I was devastated to realize that even educated women accepted the ludicrous notion that men were superior.

To accept that God does not allow women to go to *haaj* alone is accepting that God is sexist. By accepting the discrimination, they are discrediting the expression of God's justice!

Evil-spirited girl

Growing up is a great task for children. But growing up as a little girl in an Islamic culture was even more bewildering for me. At first, I felt betrayed by God, as I was constantly reminded in many different ways that God asked women to obey men. I was also told that Muslims are the only people allowed into heaven. As a child, I felt privileged to be born into an Islamic household. But the more I learnt about the oppression of women, the more I questioned the fairness of God, the more I needed to probe my entire system of belief. I was determined to find out why they claimed everybody was equal in the eyes of Allah (God), while there was extreme prejudice toward women in the name of Islam.

It was a Friday, our praying day, when I heard a new *Mulla* was to come and teach us how to read the Koran, as the old *Mulla* was fed up with my *batamezi* (rude behaviour about the Islamic teachings). On his arrival I asked him the same old question, "Could I read the Koran in Urdu?" The new *Mulla* made the same old reply... that first you have to read in Arabic, then you can read in Urdu. But the proper reading was supposed to be in Arabic. I was amazed at the ignorance. I as a child, as well as a grown-up, could not comprehend why it was compulsory to read and finish the whole Holy book in a language you have no clue about! Where is the logic?

I told the *Mulla*, "I might as well read the Koran in French or Chinese." I could see he was getting angry. I was adamant I would read the Koran in Urdu or in English to the end. My refusal to finish the Koran in a language I did not understand made me look like a witch or an evil girl. All the girls in the area as well as boys of ten to twelve had finished their Koran and here was I, who could not finish two *paras* (little books, as the Koran consists of thirty little books altogether). The *Mulla* decided to ignore me and concentrate on my brothers. The *Mulla* was talking to my brothers of the luxuries they would receive – such as beautiful women – should they follow the Islamic path.

"Would women get good-looking men in heaven if they followed the Muslim path?"

Straightaway I questioned the *Mulla*. He was furious, and astonished at my simple inquiry, as in his mind it was an outrageous question for a fourteen-year-old girl.

The look on the *Mulla*'s face was as if I had called his mother a tart! My brothers stared at me in disgust. The *Mulla* put his hands in the air, and prayed to God in his loud voice to forgive me for my evil thoughts. I was astounded that he was so outraged. The *Mulla*'s pleading to God enraged me.

For me it did not make any sense that in every area of human life these women were to obey everything they were told, but not seek any rationale in those commands. Even as a young girl I was bemused to see that all rules were in favour of men, and dominated women. When I questioned and denounced those rules, I was beaten up and called an evil-spirited girl. But no-one had a logical answer for my questions!

"There is no place in the Koran where women are given any superiority or a rank of great respect, is there?" I challenged the *Mulla*. He got angrier.

"Yes, there is," he confirmed.

I demanded he show me where exactly in the Koran it stated that a woman's place was as great as a man's, apart from a mother or teacher.

"You have an evil mind, therefore you can't see," *Mulla* replied with a devilish look in his eyes.

"Fine, but you've got a bright mind and sparkling eyes; why don't you show me the page in the Koran where it says that woman should be respected, and men should be obedient to their sisters, or even daughters?" I urged him once again.

"Anyone who is stupid enough to question the Koran is not worthy of an answer," the *Mulla* replied with fury.

"You've got no answer," I challenged him. But by this time my mother and father had entered the room. The anger and disgust showed on their faces.

"What has she done this time?" asked Mother with piercing eyes.

The *Mulla* got sombre and reasonable. "Men and women are not the same! Therefore, they do not have identical rights, but equal rights," he replied proudly, citing the example of rice and lentils, which are different vegetables but similar in proportion.

"Don't treat me like an idiot," I replied angrily.

"Go and read upstairs," Father ordered me.

My rude and outspoken attitude gave me a bad name. I was growing up in a society where children must finish their Koran by the age of 10 or 11 years: however, I was 14 years old and had not finished the holy book. Every time my parents hired a *Mulla*, I urged him to let me read the Koran in Urdu. But for some unknown reason, we, Muslims have to finish the holy book in Arabic. I could not understand the purpose. I asked my parents why shouldn't I read in Japanese or French? I was given a lousy reason that one has to read the holy book in the language it was written in. At the end I was told by people around me that I was the evil spirited girl. Most of the *Mulla* or *Mullani* (female religious teachers) simply refused to teach me the Koran. Out of seven children, I was the only child who did not finish the holy book, which gave me a bad name in society, as well as in school.

It was a cool summer evening, and we were playing in my friend's house, which was a few doors away from my home. As I went to get some water from the kitchen, I saw my friend's mother, Aunt Naima, was crying whilst looking at the family picture. I asked her why she was upset. She told me that her mother in India was in intensive care. I asked her why she hadn't gone to see her, and was amazed at her level of obedience when she replied with utter dignity, "My husband does not approve of my going to see my mother." The flood of tears kept falling from her brown cheeks, while she was drying them with her *dupta* (scarf).

Once again I, as a little girl, felt outraged as well as helpless. I was angry at these adults, who loved to dominate, while the other set of adults loved to be submissive. This ill relationship of dominance and submission was beyond my comprehension. I kept staring at her until I heard the voice of *Allah ho Akbar* (the sound of prayer) coming from her garden. I simply looked outside the window at the man who was her husband. He stood praying on the lawn, on the *janamaz* (praying mat), with his servants, the *namaz* (prayer). I hated the hypocrisy these Muslim men were carrying on their shoulders. I held on to the corner of Aunt Naima's *sari* with utter confusion. I couldn't understand how one could go in front of God when they were treating his creatures so unfairly; how could one detach humanity from religion? To me religion was, and still is, love for God and his human beings. But, at the age of nine, there was nothing I could do to ease the pain of that helpless woman, except to despise the norms of Islamic society.

The next morning my mother received a phone call that Aunt Naima's mother had died the previous night. We were all upset, but my anger had a touch of hatred as well. We went to Aunt Naima's house, and found out that still her husband would not allow her to go and pay her last respects to her mother, because he had had an argument with his mother-in-law years earlier. I was shocked to hear Aunt Naima saying, "It does not matter. My duty is to make sure my husband is happy with me; my mother's soul would not be happy if I disobeyed my husband."

Another old woman sitting next to her said with a sigh, said "This is what the Koran teaches us…righteous women are devoutly obedient to Allah and their husbands".

I was asked by mother to go out and play at that stage, as she knew that I would come up with some aggressive remarks about the status of women. I simply asked in horror "Does it really say that in the Koran?"

" Yes, in Surah a-Nisa" (*Surah a-Nisa; 34*) she proudly replied.

The room was silent; you could have heard a pin drop. I sat quietly amongst the young and old women, and still could hear the silent screams from within and around me. I knew for sure that a piece of the puzzle was missing in the law of the jungle.

THE SAGA OF AN ARRANGED MARRIAGE:
THE BRIDE PICKERS

Although I detested the arranged marriage system, as soon as I turned fourteen, a flood of people kept coming to our house to see me, as I was the oldest daughter: ready for the human bazaar. There was no way for me to escape from this undesired predicament. The sheer intensity of emotional blackmail put on me by my parents to accept the unacceptable – marrying a man I had never seen in my life before, was terrible for me.

It was one of those helpless evenings. I had just turned sixteen, and was told by my younger sister that 'a guest' was coming to meet me. However, in my frustrated state of mind, I knew that 'a bride picker was to come and inspect me'. From the age of eight, I had hated the idea of arranged marriages when I saw what my aunts were going through. The whole process of male domination was beyond my comprehension.

I looked outside the window, and felt the cool breeze touching my cheeks. I felt strange, although I could feel the fresh air, nevertheless I had the feeling of imprisonment and a sense of suffocation! I felt as if I was in a dark room gasping for air. I quickly grabbed my brother's bicycle and rode away. I still remember the thrill and rebellion in me. I was peddling as fast as I could. I did not know where I was going. Although I, like many other young girls, was forbidden to cycle, I never followed any rules that I could not justify in my own mind.

As I had no place to go, I hid myself in the old, gigantic water pipe, which hadn't been used in years. I sat there for hours and cried aimlessly. I desperately wanted to get away from the burning oppression, however there was no fire escape!

There was nothing I could do: in my eyes, the system was irrefutably biased against the female gender. I was sure that, like me, there must be several other girls who detested the Islamic system of prejudice towards women, but didn't dare speak their minds. Perhaps they were unaware of the fact that their silence and docility could be interpreted as their consent toward the ill treatment of women in Islamic society. Upon my return at about 9pm, I had no choice but to face my parents. On the one hand I was petrified to face them, but on the other I felt a great sense of victory. Mother started to shout at me. At first she grabbed hold of my hair, punched me in the head, and pushed my head onto the arm of the sofa. My nose was bleeding; my younger sister started to cry, and asked her to stop. My father, brother and other sisters stood around me like a brick wall, while Mother kept saying, "You know those people will go and tell other mothers about your attitude. How dare you run away like that! Didn't you know your parents would be disgraced?" Although Father was shouting at my mother, in retaliation she was hitting me like a boxer practising on a punch bag. I kept crying and at the same time begging my mother to stop. "*Ammi*. Please don't hurt me! *Ammi*, please stop."

It is painfully tragic that even today, after more than twenty years, writing about that day still brings tears to my eyes. I can still hear my cries: the echoes are too strong to fade away.

One of my brothers, Billo, was very understanding, but at times like these even he backed off. I remember him coming to my bedroom late that night. My eyes were swollen from crying. He told me I was fighting the system, and that I would never be able to win. With sadness in his eyes, he asked me to act like a normal girl, because it hurt him to see the violent beatings I had suffered that day at the hands of Mother, and the verbal abuse from my father.

I tried to convince my brother that the system was biased. He was calm and calculated.

"I agree, but one girl like you cannot and will not change the system. Do you think you can change the system? And if you think you can't, then stop giving *Abbu* and *Ammi* a bad name for God's sake," he retorted.

"I can't change the system, but I cannot, and will not let them dictate my life," I insisted. Billo left the room with a look of dismay on his face.

Although I didn't regret a moment of my rebellious outcry, my parents' level of intolerance was at its peak, because according to tradition I had disgraced them by not showing up in front of 'the guest'.

In 1981, my neighbour and friend, Lubna, was about to get married. She asked me if I would do her makeup for her wedding day. On the wedding day, I was horrified when she told me she didn't know the name of her husband-to-be, and stunned when she said she didn't even know what he looked like. I thought it was simply a disgrace to deprive a woman of such basic information. I was about to put her makeup on, when her aunt walked into the room and told us her husband-to-be didn't like makeup, and therefore I couldn't put any on her. Lubna was upset, but she understood the importance of pleasing her husband, even before becoming his wife! To me it was deplorable.

The concept of a woman and her sole duties has not changed for centuries. It did not surprise me when in December 2000, in London, I asked a Pakistani Muslim man, who was about to get married to his fiancée, "What are your wife's hobbies?"

He laughed at me. "I am not marrying a white girl. She is from Pakistan. 'Hobbies!' what hobbies? She's going to have kids, that's enough hobbies as it is," he replied with male chauvinistic pride. I was amazed and amused at the same time. His education could only assist him in getting a decent job!

Some of these educated Muslim men wear Western clothes and drink heavily, yet they want their wives to follow the strict Muslim code. They go to nightclubs while their wives are not even allowed to wear sleeveless blouses. Most of them are hypocrites, and the culture they belong to is hypocritical. While there are some decent Muslim men who do not pray five times a day and have nine inch beards but practice humanity, unfortunately it is the fundamentalist Muslims who control the system and give this minority a bad name.

It is shocking to see that on the one hand some of these Muslim women are intelligent enough to achieve higher mathematical and scientific degrees, but on the other, when it comes to questioning the validity of their entire system of belief, they can be as blind as bats. These women are always busy doing things to please their husbands, but never to please themselves. It is as if their sense of individuality has been eroded from their systems. But for me, even in my deepest, darkest moments, I detest the idea of serving men. I had to give up the idea of God's fairness to accept men ruling over women. My firm belief in the justice of God has prevailed, leading me to believe that the ways of a male-dominated way of living in Pakistan are unjustifiable.

CHAPTER TWO

Emotional blackmail

In an Asian society the relationship between parents and children is often a close one. Yet children have to pay the price of this undying love of their parents as it is a form of emotional blackmail. An emotional umbilical cord hangs around their neck all through their lives. Young women and girls have no say in their lifelong decisions, the most vital being arranged marriages. If the fluke pays off and the appointed husband turns out to be a good one, all credit goes to the parents for making the right decision for their daughters.

But what if the chosen husband turns out to be a nasty piece of work? The girl still has to stay in that cul-de-sac marriage and accept the fact that she was unlucky to have a cruel husband.

As a little girl in 1979, I was running around in the huge garden of our house, when I noticed the sunlight glistened on the smooth surface of the massive dinner tables, covered by clean white tablecloths. The glow on Mother's face provided evidence that special guests were expected. The servants were running around to finish their tasks. I ran to my mother and asked her who was coming.

"A man is coming to see Aunt Fouzia (my mother's sister) and if he likes her, then they will get married!" she replied with a bright smile.

"What happens if 'she' does not like him?" I held the

corner of her sari, and looked up without hesitation and asked her. My mother's eyes widened and her face dropped.

"Oh no!" she said, "That's not the way it goes. She has to accept whoever likes her! It is the man's choice whether or not to get married to the girl of his preference." There wasn't a hint of sadness in her voice.

At the tender age of eight, the prejudicial attitude towards women should not have been my concern. Nonetheless, I could not ignore the unfairness of this Asian culture of arranged marriages.

"Don't you think that it is wrong?" I asked, with a furrowed forehead. Our neighbour, Mrs Kabir, was standing by my mother's side, and immediately she intervened, leaping to the defence of Mother and of our cultural values.

"Pumpi, in Islam, men are greater than woman. You know that one woman's testimony is not enough in a murder case. You need two women to testify, but on the other hand one man's testimony is sufficient. That shows you the importance of men compared to women."

"According to whom?" I asked with great doubt.

"This is Prophet's word! The Prophet's word is God's word. It is in the Koran" She replied.

I was startled and surprised. I felt cheated by God. The one being I totally relied on, my God, had taken my pride away. I was silent, like some dead body. After a few moments I gave voice to my sense of devastation:

"This is all so stupid. It means that girls have no rights at all. Even their opinion has no opinion."

Mother was upset that I did not stop after Mrs Kabir's explanation. Mother kneeled down, plucked my cheek and twisted it as hard as she could. Then she slapped me across my face.

"Don't ever open your mouth again, if that's all you have to say. Nobody should ever question the Prophet's word!" she said.

I was outraged to see such a display of discrimination against women – and, ironically, one made by women, like Mother and Mrs Kabir. Was this Islamic society I grew up in simply hypocritical, or even demonic? I was a little girl of eight, but could see as a woman. What I saw was nothing less than the devaluation of women.

I ran to see my Aunt Fouzia, and was shocked to see her resigned to the situation of an arranged marriage. Nevertheless, she was also extremely nervous of having to go and sit in front of a stranger.

"Are you really going to sit in front of that man and his family?" I asked her.

She replied calmly. "Why? Is there any other option for women in this culture?"

In effect, Aunty was questioning the system, without expecting a positive answer.

"Do you think that it is fair?" I asked her.

"Pumpi, why don't you go and play with your friends?" Aunty asked me.

I looked at her, in the giant mirror, as she was busy putting her hair into a plait.

"Because I want to know this."

"If you can't change them, you must join them, Pumpi," she replied with a sigh in her voice.

I felt her submission to reality had cracked the mirror.

What if?

My whole image of my intelligent aunt just shattered into pieces. I could not believe that such a strong woman could surrender to such a weak argument. But the distress in her eyes told me that she was joining the show, because she had no other choice. It was incomprehensible. Look at these young bright girls, who could achieve distinctions in their studies, who can solve big mathematical problems, yet have no say in life's biggest decision. I desperately wanted to ask: what does a woman amount to, if even her most fundamental choice is determined by someone else?

I suppose the only choice of freedom that a Muslim Asian woman has is how many chapattis she wants to eat!

Anyway, the long awaited evening came, and the guest arrived with his family. My aunt had told me that she hated to be displayed in this manner. But, like millions of other girls, she had no other choice. As she was about to go and face them, I held her *dupta* (scarf).

"Why can't you just send him your photograph instead?" I asked her.

"He has to see me in person. He has to make sure that I am a fit person, I can walk and"

I interrupted and said "But people do these things when they go and buy cars, it looks to me girls are like second hand cars: just transferring the owners"

Aunt smiled at my innocent and somewhat critical reply. My younger sister Seemi did not like my answer and said "Pumpi, boys and men are made superior by God". On which note Aunty said "That is true, they are superior to girls".

"Just because they have one tiny leg extra" I said to them.

I exploded with hatred to see the exploitation of women. Surely to do so in the name of Islam was itself a disgrace to Islam – a religion that holds that all are equal before God?

Aunty gave me a hug, then held my hand and we both started to walk downstairs. She had to sit in a special place, where the man and his family could examine her properly. I was sitting in the corner watching the scene. My mother repeatedly told me to go and play outside, but I wanted to see how bad it would become.

Then I noticed my aunt's hands were shaking when she was serving the tea. The sound of a teaspoon clattering against the saucers made a rattling noise throughout the room. I hated each moment and felt disgusted. After the guests left I made a big fuss about the injustice of it all, and warned my parents not even to think of putting me through that atrocious hell.

Two days later we were in the garden. The palm trees were swinging their leaves on a cool summer evening. My head was resting on Aunt Fouzia's lap while I read about Hitler. But my aunt was looking into the sky above. Suddenly, this peaceful idyll was interrupted by my mother, who entered wearing a gloomy expression on her face.

"I have very bad news for you, Fouzia," she informed my aunt. I sat up and looked into Mother's face. It was full of grief, as if she had to break some news of a tragic accident. She pulled up a chair.

"Mr Hasan did not like you." (That was the man who had come to see my Aunt.) Then she sighed and said: "He thinks your nose was very long, plus he likes girls with fairer complexions."

I was frustrated to know that these men can go to different houses to choose a girl to be their wife, and possess the power to reject them. On the other hand, girls have no say in this process at all! We girls are human beings, after all – people with emotions of our own. Yet you would hardly realize that, judging by this sort of cruel charade.

In anger I cried out to Mother: "Our home should be a place where we should be respected by everyone, including the guests. These men should not treat other people's homes as 'car showrooms', as if they were just picking up some new vehicle!" Mother was saddened by the news of Mr Hasan not liking Aunt Fouzia. Mother did not have the strength to beat me up, like all the other times. Nevertheless, she slashed me with words by reminding me how important men are, quoting words from Koran again.

As a child, I could not understand how any normal person could believe that God, the source of justice, could be ruthlessly unfair to women.

"Then why would the Koran affirm that everybody is equal in the eyes of God?"

My questions were growing with tremendous strength, but no one was there to answer! I looked at my aunt, who was wiping away her tears. "Don't worry, I am used to it," she replied with a sigh in her voice.

"I can accept that women are weaker and lower than men. But for me to do that I need to believe that God is not fair!" I said to Mother and Aunt. Father walked in to the room, he asked me to repeat what I said and gave me a strange look, which I could not understand!

I was outraged to see the prejudicial attitude of this

Asian society towards women. I detested the fact that it seemed to make them the weakest link of the society. Aunt gave me a tight hug, as if she was embracing her own defeat at the hands of a culture that could not be defeated.

Her hug was warm and comforting. That was the day I realized the strength of a hug.

Hugs are the most powerful and only expressions of human feelings, which can be shown in times of loss, as well as joy! They are one of the simplest yet still the best things in life. At times of grief a hug eases the pain and in times of joy it enhances the pleasure.

WHAT HAS BEEN, MAY BE

I was horrified to imagine the future for my three younger sisters and myself. By the time night had fallen, I had finished the book I was reading about the savage rule of Hitler. I remember looking at the sky, with a face of consternation, and wondering. There must have been millions of strong-willed men and women in Germany, with a great sense of justice, who were against Hitler's brutality. But they had to keep quiet. It was not that those fair-minded people could not or did not want to do anything. Rather, it was a case of them not being able to afford to pay the price, to take the repercussions of their actions. I saw these Muslim women faced the same predicament! They had good intentions, but feared the consequences of their actions.

I was disillusioned about the state of mind of these women: Could this be the case in Islamic society? I was horrified to learn how ONE MAN (Hitler) could manipulate millions of people, to make them believe that he was the father, the saviour of the German nation! I was desperate to do my homework, however, my mind could not understand the thick fog of religion covering the entire fabric of Asian society.

I asked myself: "If one man can brainwash so many people, imagine the effect of millions of Muslim men in Pakistan! Maybe Muslim women do not approve of the way they have been treated, but, like the German people, they are afraid of the repercussions of their actions. Maybe it's women's silence that is allowing men to dictate as they please! And for the oppression to fester and breed."

The next week somebody else came to see my aunt, and she went through the same humiliating process. Again she was rejected, and all the while this meaningless, humiliating pattern of display was going on. Every time somebody arrived, I would stop playing outdoors and go to sit there. Not that I was enjoying the vetting process by these cruel macho men, but I wanted to give my aunt moral support. The frustration of her rejection was unbearable, but what really surprised me was the fact that she was very calm about it. The devaluation of my aunt continued, till one day she was told that a Mr Qayoum Khan liked her. He was the last of a string of potential suitors. By this time she had gone through hell and more. Once Mr Khan had made up his mind, the issue was suddenly resolved. Hence she had no say in the matter.

All she knew about that man was his name and what kind of work he did! I was petrified for my future. I shut my eyes, eager to go to sleep, but the fear of transfer from one prison to another was devastating, and robbed me of any chance of slumber.

Sweet sixteen: the first marriage

Time moved forward, unlike the Asian traditions. Eventually I lost interest in playing ring-a-ring-a-roses. I began taking great care over my appearance. Well, I suppose that's what is called sweet sixteen!

It was about 8pm dinnertime in our house. At the table my mother was giving me "the smile". The one she used to give to my aunt! Then, before the dinner was over, she revealed what she had in her mind. She told me that there was an Air Force captain who had seen me at Soraya's wedding, and he wanted to marry me! I snapped impatiently, "What?" My whole body was shaking with anger and sheer hatred. All those years I had dreaded this precise moment. I felt as if I was on death row! I was ashamed to be the part of a society that had no respect for women and their rights. Women are like flowers in the garden, and these Muslim men can pick and pluck any flower they want.

I cried, and desperately wished to escape this predicament somehow, but all to no avail. The next day, I was ordered by my father to come downstairs at 6pm to meet the guest and his family. He ordered it, as if I was one of his obedient sisters-in-law.

"Do you really think I would go and sit down like Aunt Fouzia?" I asked him.

His face tightened, and he stared at me.

"You will not be allowed to put a foot outside the main door if you don't do what you have been asked," he said.

"Pumpi, the world does not go around us; we have to follow the circle, otherwise we would be crushed underneath." Mother entered the room and said.

WHAT IF?

I shook my head in bewilderment and said to her that I would not go in front of anyone – and this was final. I broke hell's silent screams. Then the real Asian drama started to unfold, the one where the father blames the mother, and shouts that their daughter is out of control. And, naturally, it is entirely the mother's fault. At which stage the mother cries and begs the daughter to 'do it for her sake'. And of course the mother's tears often soften the child's heart, no matter what age the child is. Children strive to please their parents all through their lives.

All my brothers and sisters stopped talking to me, because of my attitude. I felt isolated in a land of guilt! I had no choice but to surrender my will power, after seeing my mother's tears. I then decided to meet the man and his family. Despite all my attempts, though, that evening I could not hide my true feelings towards this horrific system. And as I walked into the living room, my face was boiling with hatred.

I could feel hot blood rushing in my veins. The feeling of 'no place to hide, no place to run, and no strength to change the system', was eating me alive. I first stood there in silence. I was raging with a sense of hurt. There was not a single soul who could understand me. I felt misplaced: lost like a toddler in a busy shopping centre.

I gave everyone, including my parents, the suitor, and his family, a really dirty look! According to the culture, girls are supposed to greet suitors with extreme shyness. They are expected to look down demurely, and remain seated until they are asked by their parents to leave the room. But I could not put up with that nonsense. I left the room on my own accord, never mind serving tea for them! I think they should consider themselves lucky that tea was not poured on them. My actions were rebellious, and outrageous, and resulted in making my parents extremely embarrassed.

When the guests left my mother came to my bedroom and started to shout and yell at me ferociously. Father was standing outside the room, shouting at mother that she had not raised me properly. My mother's verbal abuse had no limit. That was the first time I realized that sometimes words could damage more than the metal hanger.

The way I looked at Asian culture, I felt as if I were a leasehold property, and that the lease expires at the age of adolescence, and then is transferred to the husband as a freehold. What is still hard to comprehend is the fact that mothers could compel their daughters to follow the same path. The path where they had no say, and no freedom. Don't they feel that the injustice they are putting their daughters through is unnecessary?

At last I finished at my college and was going to start university. My best friend Rubina called me over so we could discuss what subjects to take for our graduation. We were both sitting and discussing what subjects to choose when the phone rang and I was summoned by my parents to come home at once.

On my arrival, I noticed that there were a few of my father's old friends – Wing Commander Khan and his grownup children – sitting in the living room. I asked my mother why she had called for me, and she replied that she would tell me later. Soon dinner was served. But the next day I was horrified to see my mother's glowing face. To my horror, it reminded me of Aunt Fouzia's days. She came towards me and, for the first time in my entire life, my mother smiled at me.

It was extremely beautiful and heart expanding.

"Congratulations, Pumpi," she said.

"For what?" I asked.

"The Wing Commander's son has chosen you and they want the date for the wedding," she replied with smile.

However, I was like a volcano. I burst into screams.

"What the hell! Does he think he came to pick bloody flowers? So he has 'chosen me', has he?" I shouted in anger.

"You should consider yourself lucky! A man like him can get any woman," Mother responded, defending the 'bride picker'.

"But I don't like him at all! He is not at all smart," I said with disgust.

My mother gave me an angry look,

"You have no shame to talk like this. You are a girl. Who said that you are supposed to talk about men and their looks? Shame on you. Looks, height, disability, nothing has any importance for a man, other than to choose a girl. For a man it is enough to be a man. And that itself gives him the right, in the eyes of society, to get what he wants," she said.

I was outraged by the whole system. The pain of the degradation of woman was insufferable. I looked around and saw my sister Seemi, who was listening to everything.

"I don't understand why you are making so much trouble for yourself!" she said. "We all have to get married through the system of arranged marriage. Why do you think that you are so special? Why should you be exempt from the normal rules of society?" Seemi explained herself calmly, but I was livid.

"Do you think it is right for a man to peek in different houses in search of a beautiful woman?" I asked Seemi.

"Whether we like the system or not, it is *NOT* going to change," replied my sister, just as my aunt had done, so many years before.

I knew my father would not take no for an answer. He would verbally bully my mother. And that would make my mother bully me to get married to Mr Khan. At times, we have to put the future on pause, to enjoy the present. I picked up a copy of a magazine, lay down in the garden, under the massive leaves of a palm tree, where I was not allowed to lie down, as the hedge was quite short and any passing man could look at me. However, I had always sat there, under my favourite palm tree.

The rays of the sun were warming my bare feet, but all the relaxation turned into ugliness as my mother walked up. Then she asked me to go and take off my nail polish. Girls should not wear nail polish until they get married, I totally refused her order. She sat down with an angry face. "I did not even see your father's picture before I got married to him. All I knew was that he was from a good, educated family. You should consider yourself lucky," explained my mother.

"What difference does it make, whether he is from a good family or not, as long as I don't like him!" I replied.

"People look for a 'good breed' when they go to buy dogs or horses: we are talking about the human race!" Mother's words were convincing. I loved her philosophy, but still I could not agree with the philosophy of an arranged marriage.

"There is no way I am going to marry anyone, just because that is the way the system works! I want to became a lawyer and an artist and if, on the journey to my destination, I found someone, I might get married, if not I am not bothered," I told her.

I could see that she was not at all happy with what I said. She was outraged. Her tone was filled with the same detest and abuse to which I was immune.

"You have to marry this man, as I have three other younger daughters to marry."

Her voice was raised and she shouted at me hysterically. It just fuelled my enflamed emotions. I threw the magazine to one side and sat up to face her. I then asked her, with rage in every word.

"What – do – you – mean?"

Mother's reply was clear. "Daughters are parents' responsibility, but sons are independent. Therefore, whatever they do, *zamana* (society) would not say a word. But if 'they' see you are not married, they (*zamana*) would think that there is something wrong with you. That would jeopardize the future prospects for your sisters' marriages."

"Why are you so afraid of the system?" I asked Mother.

Mother was appalled to see my attitude towards the tradition, while I was bewildered at how she so glibly endorsed unlimited restrictions on girls.

Mother started to show the true colours of her hatred towards me, after seeing my rebellious attitude, by condemning my looks. It was amazingly funny, because most people used to say I looked like my mother, and it was well known that Mother was very beautiful. But she and all my siblings totally denied that I had any resemblance to Mother. Mother kept telling me that my nose was too long, when I laughed people could see all of my thirty-two teeth, therefore I should be pleased whoever liked me, referring to the recent proposal of marriage. As usual, the argument escalated into a really heated debate. Mother was criticizing everything about me, while I was condemning the male-dominated society and the twisted face of Islam.

"Do you think it is all male invention?" Mother asked me with anger.

"Of course!" I replied emphatically. "Can't you see that? It is their translation of a book. I challenge you to show me one thing that gives liberty to girls! God says everybody is equal! Did he not? Then why are men superior to women?

Mother's frowns were increasing with every second. Her eyes were biting me.

"*Shetan* (the devil) has overpowered you! You are an evil-spirited girl," she cried out.

"At least the devil believes in the existence of God!" I retorted. "Yet these supposedly Muslim men don't! Otherwise they would not treat another human being with such disrespect!" I said in my defence. Nevertheless, I was already condemned, without a trial, or a jury!

For me, being compelled into a forced marriage was nothing less than a crime! It was a crime against human feelings and respect for freedom of choice. It seemed that I had no choice; the pressure was building up on me in the form of emotional blackmail.

Those who deny freedom to others, deserve it not for themselves – ABRAHAM LINCOLN

RESCUE PLAN

Then I came up with an excellent rescue plan. I called my husband-to-be (Kamran) and told him that I would like to meet him. Although it was unheard of, because they were family friends, he did not hesitate for a moment to meet. At our meeting, I planned to tell him to cancel the wedding. That would be the easiest option. I took a friend along with me for moral support. We met in a restaurant as agreed. I was shocked to hear the way he spoke. I knew at that moment that I could not even sit with this man, never mind spend the rest of my life with him. I started to eat in the worst possible manner one could imagine, so that it would put him off. I then asked him nicely if he could do me a favour? He smiled at me.

"Of course," he replied.

"I really don't like you. Can you please get married to somebody else?" I requested.

"What is the matter?"

"I don't like the whole system of arranged marriages. I think the whole system sucks! And all because of men like you, who have the audacity to go and pick the girl they like, to be their obedient servant. Men like you are basically imbeciles and cowards," I explained.

Kamran was astonished at first. Then he thought that I was just making a joke. I informed him about my hatred and expressed my controversial views in detail. He listened to every word. "Actually I like you very much," he said. "And I can't call off the marriage. Besides, what would

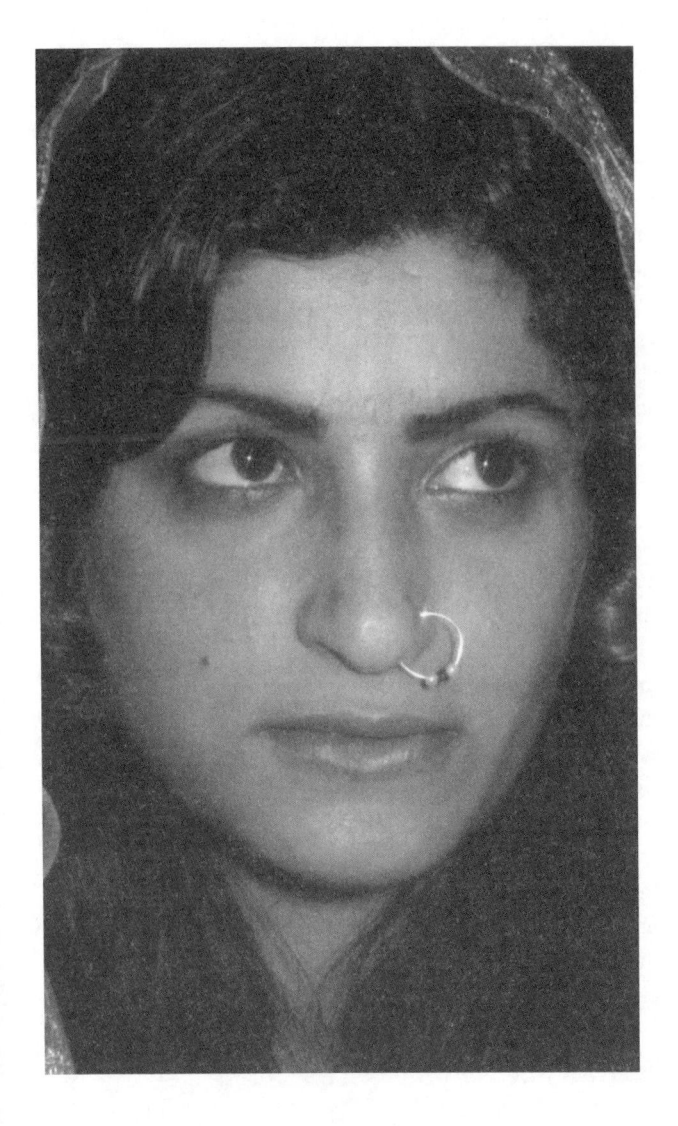

Asma Pumpi Moore

zamana say? What will my friends think of me? That 'a girl' has rejected me?"

After a long pause, he added, "My whole company will laugh at me, how could I tell them that my fiancée decided to terminate the marriage! A girl rejected me! What are you talking about? You have to go ahead with the wedding!" he said, completing his reasoning.

I realized at that moment the man was covered with an ego shell that was impossible to break. The next day was terrible as his parents informed mine that Pumpi had called their son and met him and insulted him. In a society where women are not supposed to talk to a man, this was considered a hugely disgraceful act for a girl. My parents felt highly degraded. They were enraged by my actions. The worse part came when they told me that he still wanted to go ahead with marriage. I thought that was the dead end. In the storms of life, he was the last lifeboat – but on inspection, it was a boat I found to be defective! My hopes to sail through the sea, in stormy weather, were diminishing, one by one. The flag of freedom seemed to be further away. Like a moon on a dark gloomy night, bright and shiny but unreachable.

The price of freedom

At that stage, I surrendered my weapons and decided that I would get married to him, and then soon afterwards divorce him. I forgot that if Muslim women were not given the chance to choose their life partner, why would they be given a chance to reject their husband?

The wedding day came and, as is the custom, the couple has no chance to speak to each other until the wedding night. I was taken to a well-decorated room, which had fresh red roses all around the room. The beautiful smell of fresh roses did not ease the knotted muscles in my body. Kamran's female cousins were in the bedroom (another tradition is that they sit with you till the groom arrives in the bedroom). I then decided to change my heavy clothing and tons of solid gold surrounding my neck and face. I changed my beautiful clothes and expensive jewellery. The female cousins told me that it was a sign of disrespect to take off the jewellery before the husband's feet touch the bedroom door! I was supposed to wait for him, before changing into a nightgown. But I simply took out the same old T-shirt I used to wear in my little bedroom. I started to express my views to the girls who were sitting around me, about the prejudicial system of an arranged marriage, when I noticed their facial expressions. There were imminent signs of a lack of understanding. I felt I was speaking Chinese to them, rather than good old Urdu. The lack of empathy was fuelling my anger. Finally I saw the groom, the man who had taken control of my life, without my consent; but with infinite powers invested in him by his Muslim brothers.

Kamran's cousins disappeared instantly, as he walked into the room. I showered him with my anger. I told him what a coward he was. He, like any Muslim groom, was expecting a quite obedient dummy. Contrary to his expectations, I was like an angry bull, while he was the one who was holding the red rag in his hand. I told him about the biased rules of our society and his vital part in the marriage.

My anger was at its peak, when I noticed that he was trying to hold me in his arms. I was naïve. I did not know the meaning of a wedding night, or what sex was! Nor did I appreciate that sex is an essential part of a married life. This was in Pakistan, a country where sex is the biggest swear word. The maximum intimacy of any scene children have ever seen on the television was a hero and heroine holding hands.

Well, I suppose if I was a normal Asian girl, and allowed him to discover my body, the natural phenomenon would have occurred, as it had done for thousands of years. Our grandmothers did not have any sex education, yet almost every marriage had been able to produce several children. But for me it was petrifying; the mere fact that somebody wanted to grab me was terrifying for me. I pushed him away from me. The rage of fury gave me strength. I was as angry as a wounded lioness by this time.

I was scared and confused too. I ran outside the room shouting at him. I saw several large rooms on that floor. I quickly ran and locked myself into one. He came to the door many times and knocked but I did not open the door. All night I cried and cursed the system. I just wanted to run away from that society; but regrettably, there was no escape route for girls in that orthodox culture – and there still are none....

In the morning Kamran's cousins arrived at the door and told me to dress for breakfast. I refused to come out of the room. I was determined to get out of that marriage as soon as possible. It was my naïveté, that I thought I could divorce him instantly. I stayed there for seven days, locked in the bedroom. I told him on the sixth day of the marriage that he had a chance to stop this marriage, but he did not. I told him that I was going to divorce him tomorrow! There was a massive hell, as his parents and relatives all gathered there, and thought I was 'insane'. Nevertheless, as far as I was concerned: the proof of sanity lies within the insanity of my mind!

I called one of my married friends. She told me that even she did not know anything about sex until she got married. She told me that her husband used to be very aggressive, and demand strange things like oral sex, which a girl of nineteen in our culture, at that time, had no clue about. Then one day she told one of her aunts, who told her that this was man's desire and she must fulfil whatever he asked her to do in the bedroom. I was afraid as well as disgusted to think that one could be forced to have sex in marriage.

Now looking back at the past, it seemed to me, that in a man-made culture, often, humanity seemed to be lost in the haste of applying the norms of the culture. Therefore, in the process of living, everybody becomes the victim themselves.

The next day, I called my parents to let them know that I was going to divorce him. I did not realize that through my in-laws, they knew the whole story before I opened my mouth. Mother refused to talk to me. I called her several times. Each time she refused to talk to me. Then my sister picked up the phone and as soon as she heard my voice, she slammed the phone down. I was determined to get out and go back to my home. Although I was not loved by my parents, I had great affection for my siblings.

I finally spoke to Mother, who told me that she wished that I were dead. And she told me that the only way a daughter could come back to her parents' house was inside a coffin.

Mother's remark made me numb, the feeling of being so destitute was indescribable.

I began to realize why women don't take any steps for their freedom. Quite simply, they have nowhere to go! Mother told me that I had to stay where I was sent as the wife of Mr Khan. The only way a Muslim daughter would be allowed outside a house is in an *arthy* (coffin).

The test of courage is not to die but to live!
– CONTE VITTORIO ALFIERI (1749-1803)

My whole being was shaken up by my mother's remarks. My happiness was not in their dictionary. She also told me that if I had any respect for myself, I should finish myself off.

"A dead daughter is better then a disobedient daughter," Mother said to me. Her words were enough to crush my soul. I was at the lowest point of my life. My strength was sucked up as a vacuum cleaner sucks up dust. I felt like an injured bird in a locked cage, and I could see no way out. The only way I could release that pain was to close my eyes forever, and kill myself.

I looked into each and every section of the new house I was thrown into, but I could not find any tablets. I did not know how to finish myself off. My tears had dried up by now.

I started to climb to the top floor of Kamran's house. The distance from the top floor to the cemented ground floor was enough to break my skull! I knew with the tension and pain, my brain would explode in any case. To kill myself seemed to me the logical answer. I could never forget those desperate sad moments of my life. Every brother and sister's face was coming in front of me and I was thinking that they had let me down. Then I thought about my friends, one by one, and thought that they had let me down as well. I climbed the final stairs to jump. I even asked God for his forgiveness. The loss of will to fight, the rigid society, and the fact I will always be inside this prison of a society was enough for me to kill myself. I knew deep in my heart that should I compromise, I would be killing myself each day as I live. The daily pain would be more severe than killing myself by jumping from the roof of the house I was standing on!

It was 3pm, a very hot day. The posh residents of the Defence Society, Karachi were fast asleep. The outside silence was competing with the inner silence of my being. The days are long in any hot country and this allows people to have a siesta. I was suffocated emotionally. I felt a burden of guilt that I was causing my parents such a hard time.

I remember calling my youngest sister, Parrow, who was not even ten back then and asking her opinion. I asked her, should I stay with my husband and be unhappy or should I leave him and come home?

Parrow replied after counting something in her head, "I think you should stay with your husband, because if you leave him, you will make at least forty people unhappy, by coming home you will only make yourself happy!"

She told me how sad my parents were, due to my actions.

I felt bitter about my parents; maybe it was the best way to handle me that they knew. It is a tragic fact of life that for everything a human being wants to do on this earth, he needs training, be it a doctor or a pilot. Nevertheless for the serious task of parenting, there is no way to prepare. By the time a parent learns the tools of the trade, and comes to realise the mistakes that have been made, it is too late, the children are grownup.

I strongly believe that in an Asian culture people fear *zaman* (the other people) to its maximum potential. If they put the same fear of God in themselves, the culture would prosper tremendously. It is the society that makes victims of all, including those who at first glance appear to be the chief victimizers, in this case, my parents.

I tried to look into the distant future, and all I could see was the fog of blackout. I climbed the last step and stood up on the very edge of the wall.

Then suddenly I heard a little girl's voice saying "Pumpi. I have never let you down!"

That girl reminded me of the painful moments of my childhood. The times when I was the subject of my parents' discrimination. The prejudicial attitude of my parents from the time my mother beat the hell out of me, knowing that the vase was accidentally broken by the servant, to the scary night, when I asked my father, could I lie down with him, as I was terrified just like my younger sister was, but he brutally replied: "You are not frightened, you are only jealous because Seemi's sleeping here." I felt there was a powerful soul around me. I stared at this young and brave girl, whose name was Pumpi. And that was the day when I discovered me. The re-birth of myself was the best gift God had granted me!

In my heart, I was determined to fight the battle for freedom. Deep down I knew that:

"It is not the winning of battles or war that counts.
It is the courage to 'fight' those battles that counts!" (APM)

Fight for my rights

I decided to go ahead and divorce Kamran. I knew it would be like climbing the Great Wall of China. Nevertheless, I had the new light inside my body: my whole being was re-charged. I decided to leave a note for Kamran and leave the house before he returned from work. I went to his bedroom, picked up pen and paper but my mind was racing with tension. I could not write anything: I could not even address him! Who was he? My dearest? My darling?

My capturer? I then got my lipstick out and wrote on the mirror "Sorry! I'm gone".

I took a taxi and went to C-5: my home, a broken one, but still very close to my heart.

Although I was determined to fight for my rights, but I was petrified to see the reaction of my parents. I knew throughout my childhood I had been a problem child, the black sheep of the family, but this action of mine would take their patience to its limits. I firmly believed that I was a girl and they could not chuck me out of the house. My heart was beating fast, as I entered and saw my relatives. This is very typical of our society, even if one person goes to a different city, the whole family, plus almost all the relatives would come to see him off.

My youngest sister came running to me, but was stopped

by my brother. He told her not to go near me, otherwise she would become evil, like me.

I was prepared to face the sea of hatred. I then saw Mother coming towards me and cursing me. The big living room was filled with people, but silence pierced my eardrums.

Father was still at work. But somehow he called the house just five minutes after my arrival. Mother picked up the phone then came running toward me. She grabbed my hand and said, "Get out of this house." She kept dragging me to the front door of our house. I could hear my sisters cry. I looked back with the tiny hope in my aching heart, that one, out of seven siblings would come to my rescue: but none did! By this time Mother had dragged me out of the living room and then she shut the door. I was certain that she was doing that to frighten me. I got up and knocked at the door. I knew the back door of our house would be open in any case, but I wanted to be saved any more humiliation. I kept crying and knocking at the door. Mother came out of the other room, with my vanity case in her hand, she stared at me for a second or two, but it felt like hours. Her eyes were full of rage. She threw the case at me and left. This was the moment I was never prepared for. After sitting in shock and disbelief, I went and sat at the bus stop, which was 100 yards away from the house. I sat there, kept looking at the front door of the house, still hoping that one of my brothers or sister would ask me to 'come home'. Despite all my wild actions and rebelliousness, I could not believe that Mother and Father could cut my links with the family. But they did! I think I expected too much from my siblings without realizing that all I ever gave them was embarrassment. However, my heart was filled with anger that nobody got up to say 'come home'. Well, I suppose that was one of life's major lessons: the ones you trust would hurt you the most!

I had nowhere to go. This was Pakistan, where there was no place for girls who do not obey 'men'. After a long wait, I had no choice but to take a mini bus. I was sitting aimlessly then I heard the driver say, "This is the last stop, do you know where you want to go?"

I desperately wanted to say, "I do know where I want to go! Maybe I don't know how to get there."

I then get off and took a taxi and arrived at my old classmate Sawant's house. She was horrified to see my red eyes and nose. The last time she saw me I was a bride. I told her what I had done, and the reaction of my parents as well. Sawant was frightened, she knew her parents would not approve my staying at her parent's house, as this was Pakistan, Sawant was not suppose to have her own place (this is normal, girls live with their parents till they are married). However, she managed to tell her parents that my husband had gone away on business and that was the reason I was staying at Sawant's place for a week. The whole week simply went by crying. Next week, I went to see my best friend, Rubina. She told me that in the daytime I should look for a job, while at night nobody comes to her bedroom so, after 8pm, I could stay with her in her room. The idea sounded like a perfect plan. Although Rubina never liked my wild ways, she never judged me. I was desperate to get a job and have money, as I was relying on the 'wedding money' (In Asian marriages a bride gets cash from her older relatives as well as presents, which was very handy in my case.) Although life was getting very tough, staying with Rubina was very comforting. Just the thought that there was someone who accepted me for what I was!

It was a beautiful evening, but Rubina and I could not go outside and sit in the garden like old times. Hence, we were enjoying whispering and talking, when all of a sudden her father was calling her. His voice was too close to the door, I jumped up and hid myself in the closet (as Rubina and I had planned before). Her father kept talking to her about their relatives, who were coming from India, and Rubina had to move into her younger sister's room, so the relatives could stay in her room. As soon as he left, I came out of the closet and saw the sad look on Rubina's face. I then had to find another place. Next day I went to another friend's house, her name was Shinaz Patel. She lived with her only brother and mother. Their father passed away long time ago. At first I was afraid of her brother's reaction, but could not believe his understanding when he told me that Shinaz had told him that I had not wanted to get married to Kamran in the first place. I was more amazed at his liberal thinking, than at his kind offer to stay in their flat. It was good to see that there were Asian men who were able to think along a rational path, rather than the traditional dogmatic way.

Having a place to live gave me tremendous strength to fight my battles. I went ahead to divorce my husband. However, I was infuriated when I came to know that Islamic rules did not allow me to have the same option as my husband. I could not terminate the marriage contract verbally, as my husband could have. I questioned the leading scholars in the Universities, as well as in the Mosques. Muslim *Mullas* told me that Islam gives equal rights, but not identical rights to women. An absurd justification for the biased system to demote women in society. I knew it would be difficult, but not impossible, to get freedom from male domination in my life. In 1983 in Karachi, to go and seek a divorce in the Islamic courts was not an easy task. There was no system to get any help from anybody. I went from one office to another. There were no *Yellow Pages* or *Thompson*'s directory for any information. I could not ask my brothers, as they, along with my sisters, refused to talk to me. The more they pushed me, the faster I ran!

In Public Offices in Karachi, you don't see women coming for a divorce. It was not the practice for a young woman to go and seek a divorce. This was the Islamic society, where women walked behind men. This is the society where women accept being the weaker gender. Therefore, a young woman walking into the office was unheard of. In their eyes I could not be from a good family. Hence, I was treated like a low-class woman. They could not understand my language, "I need to get the forms to apply for a divorce." For them, a woman demanding divorce papers who was married just seven days ago was a joke. It is a fact that a Muslim man can dissolve his marriage simply by saying three times, "I divorce you, I divorce you, I divorce you." Although I was unaware that even this right to divorce a spouse was given only to the man! The husband! A wife could not dissolve a marriage by mere words. Eventually, one day, I saw an old man working far behind the inquiry window of the public office. He came out from the other door.

"Daughter, these men will make fun of you, why don't you send your brother to deal with this matter?" He put his hand on my shoulder and spoke like a father to a daughter. I could see empathy in his eyes. He then told me that his son-in-law had left his daughter, with four children, and had married another girl, eight years younger than his daughter. However everybody was condemning his daughter for the divorce. I felt sorry for him, but it was his Muslim brothers who made the rules, therefore I could not sympathize as much as maybe I should have. After listening to his daughter's tragedy, I told him that I did not have any brothers who could help. He then asked me to leave the details and questions with him and he would try to find the information for me. Though he did not work in that section, he had seen me several times. And seeing the rough treatment I was getting from the staff, he decided to help me. He then asked me to come back the next day.

I arrived the next day at about 10am. After a while, I managed to find the old man. His face was very sad. He walked towards me.

"Daughter, your marriage papers have not arrived in this office and you have to apply for the divorce! My heart is weeping for you," he informed me with great sadness.

I was touched by his affection. He then cursed my husband for leaving me.

"No! No! No! My husband did not leave me. Actually I left him. I did not want to be married to the man my parents chose for me!" I explained to him.

The sympathy in his eye turned into waves of shock. He had a look of hatred on his face! It was a look of which I was all too familiar. The old man left the bench and disappeared. It was inconceivable for me to comprehend an Islamic system – or a so-called Islamic system – which allows men to finish their marriage, whether he is married for two days or twenty years, by simply saying the words: "I divorce you," three times. However, for a woman to get rid of her husband, she has to go through several stages. Why can't a woman finish a marriage the same way as man? Personally I do not think that ten or thirty years marriage should be that fragile, that it could be finished with a sentence.However, if it is 'right' for a man to get rid of his wife, equally it should be 'right' for a woman to terminate her marriage too. Nobody is asking for higher rights, but equal rights should be the essence of justice in any culture.

I was not surprised when I was told by the other office that I had to sit in front of a panel, consisting of three to four *Mullas* (religious priests). I was determined to end that marriage. I made numerous appointments, but nobody turned up on time. Then I realized that in Pakistan, men not only disrespect women, but time as well!

I carried on my battle to be free from the marriage. Then came a technical point.

As the marriage was not consummated, it should have been annulled! I could not imagine the technicalities of it! I was fortunate to meet a very loving woman, who was my friend's aunt. She was the one who told me that the marriage was null and void. I felt a great relief. However, a few days later I came to know, through my sister, that my husband, Kabir, was devastated to know that I was applying for a divorce. My sister warned me that Kabir was very determined to locate me. He called at my family home.

"She is still my wife, by law. Wherever she is, I will find her," he warned them.

I was horrified to acknowledge the infinite powers invested in men by the law. He could drag me back to his house, as I was still married to him, and there was 'nothing' anyone could do. For me it was like daylight robbery! A robbery of my self worth; I was frozen with fear. I was desperate to escape the man-made society. For me the Asian society was like quicksand!

At that stage, I knew I was better off going through the proper divorce! They would not ask me whether the marriage was consummated or not, but at least I would get a paper to declare I was not his possession anymore!

The good thing about a Pakistani marriage is that a bride gets lots of cash on the day of the wedding, as a gift. According to the tradition, that money should be given to poor people. But in my case, who could be more destitute than a young homeless girl? I kept the cash in my vanity case. I took all the jewellery given by my parents and relatives, and sold most of it. The hard times of my life have at least taught me that money can be a great friend.

It was a very hot and humid morning. Clothes were clinging to the body, like a child in horror to his mother. I decided to break free from my *Majazi Khuda* (second god), as soon as I could, before he grabbed me on the street of Karachi and got hold of me. I arrived at the massive public office. By now I had learnt my lesson, not to go from door to door. I saw a middle-aged guard in an office uniform, outside the big office. I offered him 100 rupees (Pakistani currency) and I asked him to provide me with the relevant information about the divorce procedure, in writing. At first he did not take me seriously, but as soon as I started to approach another guard, he realized that I was serious about getting the information. He then asked me to wait at the bench under the tree, while he would try to get it for me. I waited there for about thirty minutes when I saw the guard walking back towards me, a smile on his face. I was amazed, to see how efficient money could make people.

As I was counting the money, he asked me, "Why do you need this information about divorce?"

I stopped counting.

"The answer will cost you 75 rupees! Do you... want to know?" I asked him softly.

I looked at him. He smiled.

"No, no," he said to me.

I handed him 100 rupees. He was glad to take the cash. That probably was a poor man's salary for the whole month. He took the money and disappeared. I stood there and gazed at life itself! And I thought: everything is for sale, only the price may differ!

Finally, I managed to divorce Mr K. Khan. I was relieved and hurt as well, I had empathy for my parents, but an utter determination for improving my well-being. I then decided to educate myself. I had to get a job to fulfil my dreams. Therefore I joined an advertising firm called United as a model, with the help of my friend, Abida.

According to Islam, a woman has to stay indoors for

three months once the divorce is finalized. It is called *Edit*. While a man in the same position, as a divorcee, could go and dance in the street! I thought it was another of those lame excuses of Islamic misinterpretation of Islam. I was told by my aunts and other women that I should stay at home for three months. I found that absurd. I was on the catwalk in the Sheraton Hotel, Karachi, the next week. I was seen as an evil girl, who was determined to disgrace her parents. My photographs were in the Calendar magazine and I was in television commercials. My brothers stopped talking to me. My youngest sister was extremely close to me, however they (brothers/parents) banned me from coming near the house or from seeing her, as I was a bad influence on her. I was not allowed even to call home.

The following month I read that an American company was having a smile contest, nationwide. I decided to send my photograph. Though I knew I would be stoned by words if I sent in my photograph for the competition, because my divorce was finalized just last month. But I decided to go ahead anyway. Their small minds could not prevent my big dreams I told myself. Two weeks later, I was thrilled when my photograph was published in a national newspaper and I won the Colgate International Company smile contest, and received 2000 rupees! I was severely criticized for my bold actions. I was 'the trouble girl' of the neighbourhood. My actions prevented me from mixing with other girls, as I was seen as a bad influence on them.

My modelling career was going smoothly, from television commercials to calendars.

I knew my modelling must have had outraged my family. But I did not feel guilty, as it was not a glamour modelling. However, I still needed a stable job. My brothers were outraged at my modelling. But for me the thrill of the catwalk was amazing, the buzz was strong enough to make you forget every rejection and pain. The money was great but not stable. I knew I wanted to educate myself, and for that I desperately needed a job. After few weeks I found a job as a school teacher, in the White House school. I enjoyed teaching the young with their innocent questions, but soon realised that a teacher's salary would not be enough. Therefore, I decided to look for a job in a big company. Although I had no experience, I was confident that my eagerness to learn would find me a decent job. Meanwhile, one of my friends, Hameeda, found a job in a company, but her parents would not allow her to take it. So, I decided to swap my teaching job with her office job. With sheer determination, I went to the office and spoke to the manager and finally got the job at the Lakson Group of Companies, while my resignation allowed Hameeda to work in the school where I had been teaching.

After a long time I was happy with my lifestyle. My dedication to hard work was giving me hope to progress in life. I was still living with Shinaz and her family. After a few months of working in the office, I realized I could sit a distance-learning degree course. However, I needed the time off from work, but if I took the time off, I would not get the salary! Hence, I would not be able to pay for the books and the fee! I decided to tell the whole story to my boss and find out if there was any loan I could get from the company. I was ecstatic to know that I was allowed to take study leave for three weeks, plus examination days, and I would still get full pay for it. I knew it was not enough, but beggars could not be choosers! I decided to sit for a two-year course in one go. I always had a passion for questioning and reasoning, therefore I took Philosophy as my major subject for my degree. I studied day and night. My mind was expanding like a parachute. I was finally able to do what I wanted to do. God was very kind to me, He blessed me with good brains, and I was overjoyed the day I got my result: not only had I passed all my papers, I had received a first!

Survival of the fittest!

That evening I went home, to the place where I was not welcome. My father had heard the news of my graduation, plus the fact that I achieved a first class degree.

He walked towards me, I was sitting with my sisters on the lawn as I did not dare to go inside the house. Father was walking slowly towards where we were sitting. I was expecting to hear the same abuse that I was used to. However, he surprised me and my sisters by softly saying in English: "You never cease to surprise me! Well done on your result, Pumpi."

I was in disarray. Words don't fail me easily, but on this occasion I was speechless. Father then quickly walked back, leaving all of us in shocked bewilderment. My younger sister, Seemi, asked me to go and apologize or sit with our father. But my wounds were too fresh to put on a bandage, they needed to be disinfected first. I just could not bring myself to talk to him. I did not know whether I was right or wrong at that time. My sister told me how difficult it must have been for Father to hear all the abuse from the neighbours and family members. And despite all that he made the first move of communication, now it was my turn to go and take another step.

Now looking back, I know I was not only stubborn, but blind as well as I could not see my parents' wounds. I was not the only casualty, in the accident of tradition/birth.

Modelling, winning the smile contest, and graduating with a first, gave me strength and confidence in life. I just wanted to see how women on the other side of the ocean live. What was the world like, the world I had only seen in Sherlock Holmes films? Eventually, I managed to save and received a loan from the company to travel on two weeks holiday to Europe. I was excited, as it was the first time I would be acting like man, making my own plans!

Trespassing

Although I was going to London for only two weeks, my heart told me that it was the last time I would be in that office. My ticket was in my hand for May 21st 1986! The day for which I had waited so long. I decided to go and say goodbye to my parents, brother and sisters.

It was a strange feeling, when I entered my childhood home. I knew that I was not welcome there. And worst of all was the fact that there was nothing I could do to make them welcome me. I felt I was trespassing, although this was my childhood home: the place where I had learnt my first steps and my first vocabulary. A part of my being was breaking from me, bit by bit. I was walking slowly, with injured heart and soul.

I felt like a tree that had been cut down, but with its roots still in place. It was my birthright to be there! I started to walk upstairs, as all the bedrooms were upstairs in our house. I was climbing upstairs, like a thief. My heart was aching with pain, while the tears were kissing my cheeks. I could smell my sweat on the walls of the landing. I could hear echoes of the joyful cries of my brothers and sisters. There were seven of us. The house was like the "tube station at rush hour" at times. I went to my little room. The walls in my room were still the same as they were the day I left! And the same as the day I had to get married. I sat on my bed, and clung to my pillow: my friend on whose shoulders I had shed so many tears. I remembered the numerous days sitting on my bed and writing letters, in my childhood, to God. I looked around, at the picture of Abraham Lincoln surrounded by those of Indian film stars. They were still there. So were the golden words of Socrates, in my handwriting on the wall, which read:

"I know nothing, except the fact of my own ignorance!"
– SOCRATES

When my parents knew that I had actually bought a ticket for England, they were absolutely outraged. Their curse was unremitting. They could not believe that I could even think of going to a country on my own! But for me it was my dream to be at the Karachi Airport: not as Ms Hameed or Mrs Khan BUT as Pumpi.

COLD AS ICE!

I went to see my father and apologized for my behaviour. But he did not care for my emotions, as usual. He was reading a book. He did not put the book to one side to acknowledge that I was in the room. He made me feel as if I did not exist at that moment. Far away a Carpenters' song was playing. The words were pretty appropriate for that time. "I was the black sheep of the family! You tried to teach me right from wrong." A stream of tears rolled down my cheeks!

He simply shouted behind his book, at the highest pitch of his voice: "Get out of this house: you are dead for me!"

When my aunt learnt about my travelling plans, she told me that I would be called a runaway girl, if I went as I planned. I was glad that nothing was altering my firm decision. I told them that I would rather be called a runaway girl, than the slave of a meaningless tradition.

A young girl, a divorcee, travelling alone to a foreign country, to enjoy life – this was another slap to my parents' sense of honour, as the Islamic culture does not allow girls even to go ALONE to God's home Mecca for worship! Therefore, it was a great insult for my family. But I could not understand the degradation of girls. From my perspective, it was self-inflicted disgrace for them. My parents and brothers tried in their own ways to stop me going abroad. All types of threats were made against me. But I had made up my mind to peek into another world.

I decided to see Mother to say goodbye. My sister, Roomi, told me that she was in the back garden. I walked there and saw her sitting on a chair, her back towards me.

For several moments I stood still, behind the chair, but it seemed like a century. I was deeply, deeply hurt by both of my parents. But this was the time to say goodbye, and I had to do it.

My tears were silently rolling down on my face. I did not know what kind of a verbal abuse I might receive at the hands of Mother. I started to bite my lips. My hands were shaking. I plucked up courage.

"I am sorry, *Ammi*!" I whispered in a soft tearful voice.

Although I wanted to say million more words, my face was wet with my tears, and my throat was as dry as a desert.

Mother jumped out of the chair. I quickly moved backwards, and put my hands on my face. I was mentally prepared for a beating, so I felt numb when I found myself in my mother's arms. Her grip was very tight. I could not believe that I that she was hugging me in her arms! The only place where every child feels safe. Loved and secure, irrespective of their age. She was crying bitterly. I was puzzled. Was she was crying for the way she had treated me over the years? Or was it simply a mother's intuitive feeling: that my child won't be back for a very long time. I could see in her tearful eyes that she did not want me to go far away.

But I suppose, emotionally we had many miles between us. An entire lifetime would not be enough to cover those untravelled distances!

Interim thoughts: the chimera

In my opinion, Islam, like any other religion, is ultimately based on blind faith. Teachers and parents ensure that young minds do not doubt the principles of Islam. They are well aware of the fact that if the mind doubts, the brain seeks knowledge. I kept questioning the morals of the society and its prejudices. My rebellious attitude was soon well known in the area and, by the time I was 15, many parents barred their children from playing with me.

Now, as an adult, all I can see is that many Muslim men have used the word of Islam to oppress women and make them feel inferior. And the most painful part is that most women in Islamic societies have accepted male domination as part of their religious doctrine and don't question the authenticity of these jurisdictions. In my opinion, Asian Muslim women should fight for their birthright of freedom. Muslim women should understand that they do have basic human rights, and that those rights do extend beyond the kitchen and labour ward.

It is a great tragedy that Muslim men can get shelter as asylum seekers on foreign soil when they flee persecution. Yet Muslim women, who in the name of tradition suffer abuse from childhood at the hands of their own families have no place to seek refuge in another country, because abuse of women is not considered a crime.

It seems to me that Muslim women are entangled in the fabric of religion. Hey cannot escape tradition. I often wonder where they would go if they stepped out of their restrictive boundaries. So we need a 'social circumcision' in order to reveal the more compassionate side of male-oriented society. What the skin is to the body, so religion is to society. Remove the 'religiosity' of rigid dogmas and misinterpreted traditions, and you lay bare that sensitive and caring aspect of humanity. Muslim men should take some time to look at their actions and ask themselves whether or not they have been fair to women. We need men to have a change of heart. Men have to be more responsible for their actions, rather than hiding behind religious dogma.

CHAPTER THREE

London 1986
A thousand-mile journey starts with a single step.
– *Chinese Proverb*

It was Wednesday morning, May 21st 1986, when the captain of the Air France flight announced we were flying over the English Channel, but for me it felt as if I were flying over the moon. At approximately 8am, the plane landed at London's Heathrow Airport. I felt as Neil Armstrong must have when he stepped onto the moon! It was a giant leap for a girl like me!

Although I had waited for this day for a long time, I could not control my emotions. I was crying and laughing at the same time. My heart was thumping at a tremendous rate, as if every Asian mother were knocking at my heart with sheer anger, and telling me it was wrong to be without a father or brother. I could not believe I had travelled all alone! The sense of freedom and victory taken for granted by many Western girls was a major accomplishment for me. It was the first time I had ventured outside the country of my birth. I was like a prisoner on parole!

In the eyes of almost all Muslim Pakistanis, I was a 'runaway girl'; a rebel, daughter of Syed (Prophet's descendent) who had disgraced her family. Nonetheless, I was not concerned about their opinion, because this had no value in my eyes. I was trying to break the chain of a disproportionate way of living and move on.

What if?

In those days visas were issued upon arrival, and I was given a four-week one at Heathrow Airport. I had the address of a friend's cousin to go to in St John's Wood. I took the famous British cab; I knew I was in the driving seat. I was amazed to see the super organization in Britain – a place where women live above ground, not under the shadows of their fathers or brothers. During the second week of my stay, I was travelling on a bus when I asked an Englishman seated beside me whom I should contact to get information about furthering my education. I remember vividly that he was quite shocked: I had disturbed his reading, as well as asking my question. Perhaps, for a moment I had forgotten I was no longer in Pakistan, where we talk to anyone, and disturb whomever we want.

"Your college should help you," he replied softly, after glancing at me. I explained to him that I had only arrived in London the previous week, after which he gave me the relevant information. As soon as I got off at Oxford Circus, I located a public telephone and called the Home Office. I was overwhelmed to know that my visitor visa status, only valid for four weeks, would automatically change to student visa status as soon as I was accepted into a college.

Once more, I was delighted to know I could spend time away from the conservative Islamic society. My aim was to educate myself and break away from the 'arranged marriage saga'; my desire was to be independent. Although I had been living in an extremely hot country, it was under a very cold atmosphere. However, the chilled walls of home could not freeze my burning desire for freedom.

I was staying with my friend's family in their flat in St

John's Wood. I called my sister in Pakistan to inform her of my whereabouts. The next thing I knew my parents' ego was at its peak. They sent me a demand, written by my sister, that I must go and stay with my mother's sister, Meeno, in Brixton. I was shocked to see that my parents could still control me, even from such a distance. Had I been a man they wouldn't have been bothered about my not staying with family they personally didn't know. I had to go and stay with my mother's sister, knowing that if I pushed my parents and brothers any further they would probably kill me eventually. I had no choice but to find Brixton and move in with my aunt.

It was a lovely cool evening when I arrived at their house in Brixton. I knocked at the door of the house in St Lawrence Place. I wore a beautiful, long dress, but my head and chest were not covered like a good Muslim girl. When Aunt Meeno opened the door, she gave me a bitter look. She told me that my parents had asked her to give me a room until I finished my studies. She then gave me a list of chores to perform. It came as quite a shock to me, as I never had to do work at home; we always had servants to help us. Aunt Meeno had stepdaughters who told me to listen to everything, and then do exactly what I wanted to do. They told me they smoked, drank, and even took drugs, but in front of their parents, they had to act like good Muslim girls. They told me to change my clothes at a non-Muslim friend's house. That way everybody would be happy.

It took me a long time to comprehend that this hypocrisy was, and is, a vital part of our Asian Islamic culture in Britain, as it was in Pakistan. As people don't stand up and demand justice and freedom, everybody is frightened of everybody else, in the name of the *zamana* (society). Most Muslim men pray *juma* prayer on Friday, and drink religiously in the evening, although Islam strictly forbids alcohol. Some girls pretend to go to the library to finish assignments, but in reality they are having sex with their boyfriends in the backseats of cars. Meanwhile the *zamana* forces the pretence that Muslim daughters are virgins and husbands and sons don't touch alcohol. Everybody is afraid of what others might say! The fear of humiliation seems to prevail over freedom and justice.

Follow the tradition or get out

It was early morning in July 1986. By now I got the admission in the City of London College. I was happy to get an admission to study a diploma course in Marketing and Advertising. My college was in Aldgate East, however, I was staying at Brixton.

As I was getting ready for college, I fell and broke my wrist in Aunt Meeno's house. Life was hard enough as it was, but working and studying with one hand was almost impossible. Aunt Meeno's attitude was full of hatred, because of my total refusal to accept a man of my family's choosing. In hindsight it must have been hard for her to comprehend my outrageous attitude, as her first husband had divorced her, and here I was, a bright, young girl, almost the same age as she had been, challenging every norm of Islamic society. She had no idea what her daughters were up to, therefore she thought I was the only bad influence in her house. She told me she had three daughters, and that my refusal of an arranged marriage would encourage them to break with the culture also. Aunt Meeno's voice was full of rage and anger. That night she told me I should accept the fact that there was no place for a woman, except in her father's or husband's house; in other words get married to an old man, or go back and be a schoolteacher for the rest of my life. She left the room after giving her order. The misery of the day unfolded into the night. I lay down in my box room, my shelter at the time. I closed my eyes, which was far easier than closing my mind! It was about 9:40pm the same evening when Aunt Meeno walked into the room. She was like a lion getting ready to pounce on a helpless deer. She started to yell at me again, her eyes almost popping out of their sockets. My hands were trembling, and tears were falling.

"Pumpi! You now have two options. There's a man with four kids who works at the local travel agency. He's looking for a wife to look after his kids. He saw you in the kitchen yesterday."

I interrupted her before she could tell me the second option.

"But the only man who was in the kitchen yesterday was that Chacha man, the old, fat uncle," I replied. Her face turned red with anger.

"Do you really think a bachelor, a young man will marry you? You are a divorcee; you'll get proposals from fifty- to fifty-five-year-old men, who are widowers or have left their wives. You should consider yourself lucky that he liked you. You and I both know he could easily get a sixteen-year-old bride from Pakistan," she replied angrily.

A boulder of despair had demolished my shrine of hope.

Filled with bitterness towards the male chauvinistic society, I smiled nervously at her. She proceeded to tell me the second option. "Pumpi."

"Yes, Aunt," I replied with a sense of bewilderment.

"Get out of my house," she demanded. Aunt Meeno knew I didn't have any other place to go. However, this was not the first time I had received a threat of this kind: this was the same sentence my mother had uttered when I left my Asian marriage, the same command my father made when he asked me to get out of the family home. But tragically the same sentence has the same pain of rejection. However, I was determined not to let my exclusion get in the way of my crusade toward liberty, so I took the rejection as the key to a new horizon. Aunt Meeno grabbed my little suitcase, ran downstairs, and threw the case outside. She then ran back to my room, pulled my hair and shouted at me.

"Now you know why women in Islam have to behave in a certain way; because they know there is no place for them except in their father's or husband's house. My first husband divorced me; I had to marry a man fifteen years older than me, with three children from his previous marriage, while my ex-husband got married to a girl thirteen years younger than him. This is our culture, you cannot deny it," Aunt Meeno shouted from the half-open door. "You are absolutely right, I can't deny it. I acknowledge that is how our culture operates, thanks to *Mullas*. But I do not have to accept this primitive and inhuman culture, just because I was born into it. Unethical norms of a society do not make the culture right. Just because the norms have been followed for donkey's years, it doesn't mean those norms are justifiable," I replied with sheer hatred and anger. Aunt Meeno was furious at my explanation, and pushed me away with brute force. Since I only had one hand to balance myself, I fell onto the hard floor. "You don't believe in Islam, no wonder you don't like anything the society says. You are evil. You will destroy my daughters and give my family a bad name, just like you gave your parents a bad name. Just get out," she declared wildly. "You think Islamic rules are twisted rules. You have a twisted mind," she continued.

My stomach felt a hard blow as she kicked me. I tried to get up several times, but her brutal kicking didn't stop. With my right hand, I clutched the bottom of her sari. In the process of pulling myself up, her sari fell down! Aunt Meeno was furious. I was standing at last. She was too busy with her sari to stop me. She then told me I had twenty minutes to get out of her house. Even the Mafia gives twenty-four hours notice! I thought to myself. I was petrified of my uncertain future. I had been in England for such a short time, yet I was supposed to know my way around already. Since I didn't have any other place to go, I begged her to let me stay. But she was my mother's sister; mercy was not in her blood.

My tears were like the river Nile when it broke its banks.

"You have a cousin in Wimbledon. Why don't you go to her?" she suggested.

By then it was 10:40pm. Aunt Meeno picked up the rest of my bags, and flung them out of the room. She looked at me.

"Are you leaving? Or do I have to throw you out as well?" she asked. "Get out or do I have to throw you out, *Kutya* (bitch)?"

I had no choice. My mind was about to explode. Aunt Meeno got hold of my hand, and dragged me downstairs toward the front door. Her steps were as fast as my helpless, frightened heart. I had to run with her. I hated every moment of that July. Aunt Meeno opened the door of her house, and pushed me outside. I have never felt as humiliated as I did at that moment. Falling on the doorstep, I cursed her from the bottom of my broken heart. Outside the rain was constantly pouring down. I had a fractured wrist. I had only been in England for four weeks. Everything was unfamiliar. I got up, and looked up at the sky for a sign of God's existence. I was as petrified as if I were facing death; the certainty of an uncertain future was sucking each drop of my blood. I just had nowhere to go! Deep down inside, I knew they wanted to break my spirit to a point where I would do anything they wanted me to do. Aunt Meeno grabbed my hand; I could not break the clutch. I had nowhere to go! No one to call! Even God's extension was engaged. I had no choice but to leave Aunt Meeno's house, but where would I go? The fracture in my left arm rendered me unable to carry all my bags. With my right arm, I picked up one of the cases, leaving the other at the front door where Aunt Meeno had thrown it.

I was angry at the whole of the Islamic world. I came out onto the lonely road of life.

A severe feeling of dejection was burning inside me like a rapid infection. I did not have a shoulder to cry on, nor did

I even have a way to dry my tears, as one hand was fractured, and the other held my bag. I tried to console myself with the fact that at least I was alive. But then again what is life without living? Is killing your desire life? Is fighting for freedom life? Questions kept coming to my mind, but I was left without any answers.

Aunt Meeno was a religious person, a woman who would not miss a prayer, who fasted regularly during *Ramadan* (a religious month). At times like that one wonders what good religion is, if it can't teach you to love a fellow human being: a creature of God. I looked at my watch; it was about 11:05pm. I looked back at Aunt Meeno's house, but the door was closed. I stood alone. Darkness and loneliness wrapped around me like a blanket. The high winds of injustice made the candle of hope in my heart flicker. I wasn't certain of anything, except that I wouldn't give up my fight for liberty!

I walked through the streets of Brixton for a while, with fear spreading inside me. I was like a little kitten, terrified of every little sound or movement. I went to the Brixton tube station, which was about twenty-five minutes walk from Aunt Meeno's house. I had no place to go! I had ultimate freedom, but its cost was utmost rejection. There were floods of people coming out of Brixton station, but the fact that they ignored a young girl, late at night, sobbing bitterly, told me something very chilling about Western society. It took me a long time to accept the ignoring aspect of English culture! You see! But you don't see anything!

The night was getting darker and darker. The streets of

Brixton still bustled with people. Small, shady dealings were being carried out on the street corners. The emotional stress had exhausted my strength. I walked slowly towards Aunt Meeno's house thinking I'd ask her to forgive me. It took me a long time to walk back to her house. I was about to knock, when I realized that I couldn't lower myself!

Don't compromise yourself! You're all you've got!
– JANIS JOPLIN

LIFE ON THE STREETS OF LONDON

The streets of Brixton were getting dark, much darker than any other night of my life. I knew I had to find a place where I could spend the night; I had no knowledge about hostels, or any other kind of accommodation, but I was determined to survive, and amazed at my own strength to carry on! I could not bow to Islamic traditions; I strongly believed they were the extensions of male testosterone.

It's ironic that although I knew I was alone in the battle, I never felt lonely. The enigmatic aura of my Lord was always around me. I started to walk towards the park. From a distance, I could see houses and their lights. It was pitch dark, and almost impossible to see if anybody was there. I couldn't see my hand in front of my face. My whole body was shaking with cold and fear; I didn't know whether it was the fear of the known or the unknown! I sat on the concrete path of a little park in Brixton, surrounded by a blanket of fear. My stomach aching with hunger, I curled up into a foetal position. The last thing I had eaten was supper at Aunt Meeno's house at 7pm. I had no choice but to question myself! Is it worth it? Giving up my home, where a servant called when the food was ready to be served, and I could call a maid to bring me a glass of water. I never even knew the price of washing powder or soap, as everything was provided for us. The only job we had to do was push the dining room chair back under the table after finishing our dinner. If we didn't do that Father would shout, "What do you think this is? A restaurant?"

Then I thought about my husband's house where there had been servants also. I simply didn't know how to fry an egg, or even how to boil water. I started to cry in the lonely valley of life. I had to reassure myself that if the days of comfort hadn't lasted, neither would the days of discomfort.

Better to reign in hell than to serve in Heaven!
– JOHN MILTON, *Paradise Lost*

After a while the rain stopped. I took out some clothes from my bag and made a pillow, thinking I'd sleep on the concrete ground. But unfortunately it was extremely hard. I put the clothes back into my bag, and tried to use it as a pillow, but it wasn't big enough. I just took a rest on the bag, and in the darkness waited for morning. The whole night was like a nightmare; I knew life was going to be a struggle, but I didn't know it could be that uncomfortable. Early in the morning, I felt half asleep, and half awake. My tears had dried, and my eyes were closing with fatigue, I heard some strange noises coming from the bushes. I was frightened to death.

The mere thought that I had nowhere to hide or run to was enough to make anyone uneasy. I put my hand into my mouth, biting my nails. Then suddenly a timid cat came out from the bushes. I felt relieved and happy to have a companion. She gazed at me. In the dark night her eyes were like that of a tiger. I waited anxiously for the morning. I didn't sleep all night; the fear alone was enough to keep me awake.

In the morning my whole body was stiff. I couldn't believe that I had spent the night on the streets of London. A city I was so excited to see. I was more shocked to find myself safe, with both my gold chains still around my neck. I felt feverish. My whole body ached. However, there was a sense of relief that I had not surrendered!

I walked to the high street and found a cafe where I had a big breakfast. My bones were aching, but my heart was whimpering that the journey of life had just begun. I registered as a student at City of London College.

I called my sister in Karachi and got my cousin's number from her. I called my cousin, Rashida, who didn't seem very happy to hear from me. In Asian culture, if you aren't somebody's wife you have no place in society. A divorcee does not get respect at all. She only gets the stigma, and criticism from everyone. I remembered Mother saying to me that as a divorcee people will spit on you, but if you were a widow people would have sympathy! That just shows how shallow people in that culture truly are! My cousin, Dr Sima Shan, told me that she currently had visitors, and so had no room for me. However, I knew that if I were accompanied by a husband, I would have had red carpet treatment. I had no choice but to go back to that pitch-dark corner for the second night. I thought for a moment that I should have told my cousin I had no other place to go; she might have been more sympathetic. But my pride didn't allow me to ask for pity. I didn't attend any of my classes, as finding food and shelter was my primary concern. I went back to Brixton. It was only 5:30pm, too early to lie down or sit there, so I decided to sit in the tube, because at least it had a cushion. I then had to walk back to the station. Rush hour was at its peak, but gradually the flood of people slowed down, and the last stop came. When the guard shouted, "All change," I felt once again as if I was homeless! Then I realized I could jump into the other train, which was going far... just to pass the time in a safe place. I did this many times, and I was getting tired of sitting. But beggars can't be choosers! My back ached, but it didn't break, as it had a companion – my heart!

By now it was nine-ish in the evening, and I decided to head for my dark, little corner in Brixton; my temporary shelter. My second night on that corner was a little bit better, or perhaps it was the sense of familiarity that made the place less fearful. I felt confident walking there, but it was 11pm by then. Apart from the occasional hiss of my insect companions, the place was as silent as a graveyard. I put down my bag, and waited patiently for the timid cat. It wasn't long before I saw the same bright eyes coming toward me. After a while I smiled. She came close to me, and brushed herself against my lap. A wave of pleasure ran through my body. Then all of a sudden it started to rain, and the little cat ran away. I prepared myself for a long, wet night. I simply wrapped the blanket around myself, and prayed to God to keep me in his safe hands. The night was getting colder, and I was suffering from a severe migraine. I took out two Aspirins, and then swallowed them with water. I did toss and turn, but compared to the previous night, I had a spell of short naps. By now my body was not only aching, my eyes were very hot as well. I didn't even have the strength to get up. I knew I was coming down with a fever, as I felt extremely weak and thirsty. I smelt like a pig. The morning was getting brighter and brighter, unlike my destiny. I saw children in their uniforms passing by me. I knew I had to knock at somebody's door. But then I realized I could have another Aspirin and I might get better. I took out two Aspirins and the bottle of water. Inside my soul I was going through hell; this battle for freedom was tearing me apart. I remembered that the only time my mother was kind to me was when I got ill. Mother used to put her healing hands on my forehead, and rub in the good, old Vick, with the message 'it will be all right' in her eyes. For a long time the thought of being ill was my ultimate desire, just so my mother's hands could be on my forehead, and her eyes could see me with love. When I was a little girl, there was pleasure and a sense of security in being unwell.

I felt like an abandoned graveyard. People walked past where I was half-sitting and half-lying down. But nobody wanted to bother; nobody wanted to know what had happened to this young girl. The climax of Asian society and Western culture were at the extreme. Back home my neighbour would walk in and ask my mother to control me; here I was on the street and nobody's mother even stopped for a second glance.

After a while I sat up and dragged myself to the bench. I managed to have a spell of naps. I remember being woken up by a fat, smelly woman, who said to me, "Where do you think you are, at home? Move over." She smelt of urine and stale beer. I felt like vomiting. I dragged myself back to the spot where I had been before, at which point it started to pour again.

I remembered there was an old Irish woman, who used to stand at her green gate with her daughter, Margaret. They called me Sunshine as I passed their gate. I spoke to them twice; once when they asked where I was from, and once when they said, "Hello," as I passed their door. Their house was just before Aunt Meeno's house. I knew I needed urgent shelter. My whole body was shivering. I had no physical strength left in me. I felt as if I was going to die, and for some reason I didn't want to die in my dark corner. I grabbed my rucksack. It felt very heavy, because of my lack of strength. So I walked slowly, dragging the rucksack behind me.

The weather was dark and gloomy. I wore jeans and a blouse, both of which were soaked through. My blanket swept along the ground. I wasn't even sure which one was their house. I walked down the road, and luckily recognized the green colour of their door. I dragged my bag to the stairs; it was like lifting up an elephant. I knocked on the door, feeling like an escaped prisoner. I heard *tuk...tuk...* and a middle-aged woman appeared and said, "Oh! Jesus Christ, are you okay?" By that stage I was so weak and emotionally drained I couldn't even speak.

The woman was as kind as Mother Teresa. She made me soup and toast, and took me to a small room and asked me to change my clothes. By this time, my mind was numb.

She then said something I didn't understand, and disappeared for a while. When she returned she had something in her hands. I lay half dead on the chair next to the bed. She pulled out my blouse and handed me a long cloth. I don't remember how she managed to change my clothes, but she did. My body was extremely hot, and my head was spinning like a yo-yo. I was in a state in which I would have taken anything to feel better. I was very fortunate to have had Peggy and her daughter, Margaret. Every fibre of my body had been praying for someone to help me. Miracles do come in different shapes and sizes. I remember her saying something to her daughter, who then disappeared. The next thing I remember was Peggy giving me a tablet.

A ray of sunshine piercing the curtain gave me the sense that it was morning. I opened my eyes and looked around, finding myself in a strange place. I was delighted to see four walls around me, feel a pillow under my head, and a warm blanket surrounding me. Although it gave me a sense of security, I couldn't understand how I had ended up there. I was baffled. The door opened and a pale-looking woman with a smile on her lips and in her eyes entered the room. She said, "Hello, Sunshine, how are you? You gave us quite a scare last night. Maggie told me she saw you staying at St Lawrence Way. Are they relatives of yours?"

I could barely speak as I still had a fever. Peggy told me to get some rest, and then left the room. I woke up the next day, after having slept for a good forty-eight hours. I then realized what had happened and how I ended up there. I stayed in Peggy's house for six days, and will never be able to repay her for her kindness.

The first few days I was quite ill, but after that I stayed because I had nowhere else to go. Even after all these years, my heart still prays for her, and is still grateful for her kindness on that fateful night. When I got better, I started college. I also decided to get a job, and realized I would have to miss class again. I always had a passion for knowledge. I was weeping inside, but I knew if I attended classes, I wouldn't be in the right frame of mind to listen anyway. My first priority was to find a place to stay! I called my so-called cousin, Dr Rashida Khan, but every time she pretended she was unable to hear me, and then put the phone down. She forgot that determination was my middle name! I kept trying and trying. Finally I got her. She asked me to come and stay with her. I arrived there, but her attitude was quite obviously rude. I felt as if I were a burden on her. She told me that if I wanted to stay in her house, she would have to sack her maid. I didn't understand what she meant, so she explained that England was very expensive, and that nobody did anything for nothing. I would have to do the cleaning and dishwashing in the house. I didn't mind at all. There was one problem, though. I had never even washed so much as a cup in my life, as I had grown up always having servants and maids. I managed to vacuum the carpets, but I didn't know you had to empty the bag; therefore I didn't do the cleaning, and told her the vacuum cleaner didn't work. My ignorance infuriated Dr Rashida, and she hurled a lot of verbal abuse at me. Her eyes were full of anger, and reminded me of my mother's. She shouted at me, "If you were such a princess of luxury, why did you bother to come to this country? There aren't any servants here! Don't you know that one has to empty the bag?" She wore a beautiful sari, and when she bent down to open the clip, her long plait fell over the bag. She shrugged. When her anger reached its climax, she simply threw the bag at me. I was watching what she did, so I'd know what to do the next time, and then all of a sudden there was dust everywhere; it was a slap of dust full of humiliation. I felt degraded and guilty that I had made her so angry. "They couldn't tolerate their daughter, so they expect the relative to sort her out. Why can't you go back and do what normal girls in Pakistan do? Tell me why you can't be like them?" she shouted at me. She walked downstairs, the anger raging from her pores.

"What is so special about you that you don't want to follow thousands of years of tradition, Pumpi?" she asked.

I didn't reply. It wasn't that I didn't have answers to her petty questions, but I knew she wouldn't be able to understand the logic behind my actions. I was deeply saddened that I had to go from one house to another, and nobody was ever happy to see me. Dr Rashida's attitude toward me was outrageous. I felt my ego slashing into pieces, and dropping to the floor. She had a very big Edwardian house, but as a divorcee one has no status in the Asian society. In our male chauvinistic society, you are either somebody's daughter, or somebody's wife. If you are disowned by your parents, and have no husband's name after your name you are a low-class girl, and society refuses to give you any respect. I was given the loft, which was not even converted. It had lots of old suitcases, accompanied by cobwebs. In one corner there was a mattress in an upright position, old shoes were scattered everywhere, and heaps of metal, probably from car spares, lay in another corner. I didn't mind. By this time I knew I would never get respect from the shallow people of the sick Asian society, because of the stigma of being a divorcee, and my unstoppable courage in speaking out about the prejudicial attitude towards women. It was my frightening experience of a Brixton corner that was a constant reminder that I had to be a slave, or else face living on the streets of London. In the morning, Dr Rashida's eldest son, Amid, showed me their beautiful house. Each room was like a five-star hotel room.

"I wonder why Mama sent you all the way up there, when there are four rooms nice and clean downstairs?" Rashida's little boy asked.

It was 5:30pm in the evening. I was studying in the attic, when I heard Rashida opening the front door. I rushed to the kitchen, remembering that I had forgotten to clean it. It was difficult enough to do housework with two hands, but with a fractured wrist it was hard to do anything, plus I was too involved with my studies. Rashida walked toward me, and told me my parents had sent a summons for me to go back to Pakistan, or else they would disown me. I told her I had no plans to go back to prison!

"I won't go back and marry another Asian man. I want to educate myself and get a job," I said. Before I had even finished my sentence, Rashida flared up, because in the Asian culture girls are not supposed to talk like men!

"What the hell are you planning? Have you ever seen an Islamic woman living alone? What will the *zamana* (society) say? You will disgrace not only your parents' name, but our name as well. GET OUT OF THIS HOUSE if that is what you are planning!" Rashida ordered. Her eldest son, Amid, who was about fourteen years old, walked into the room. "Mama, Pumpi *baji* doesn't have anywhere to go! It's a free country; why can't she express her opinions?" he said.

Rashida was furious and outraged, not only to see that her son was taking my side, but also that he was making a logical statement.

"Amid, please leave this room now," she ordered her son. Amid left the room.

"Now see how quickly you have influenced him. You have an evil spirit in you, preaching against Islam. Meeno was right that you will exploit our children's minds," Rashida continued.

"You mean open their minds!" I whispered. Rashida came closer, and bent over me, as she was taller than me. Her face was too close to me; her nose by now touching my nose, her eyes were popping out of anger. She gave me a venomous look.

"What did you just say?" she asked.

By that stage I knew she had already decided to ask me to leave her house. I wanted to open her eyes to the prejudicial attitude of the Islamic society! But I knew she had chosen to keep on the blinkers handed out by Islamic men. Rashida asked me to apologize for what I had said.

"I said what I believe, and what I believe I must stand up for," I replied. Then she said, "Either apologize or get out!" and left the room.

I closed the door of my room, but in my heart I knew another door was closing for me. I clenched the pillow. My tears simply rolled down and were absorbed by the pillow. I lay down on my bed and stared at the blank ceiling, a reminder of my blank luck. I was very frustrated about the situation I found myself in. I felt as if I were on a treadmill – walking for hours but going nowhere! I kept crying and thinking I should be enjoying my youth, yet here I was each night, having to fight another battle.

Our greatest glory is not in never falling, but in rising every time we fall – CONFUCIUS

It was early in the morning. Outside the birds were singing, but inside my heart was crying. I started packing my little suitcase and rucksack. My eyes were sore from crying all night. I was petrified to go back to my corner in Brixton, but I had no other place to go. I went to City of London College. After attending classes, I passed the time by sitting in the tube, as I had no friends to go to, nor any family to stay with. I stayed in the tube till the driver announced, "ALL CHANGE!"

My dreams of having a life were not being realized. In the train I controlled my tears, as I could see the eagerness on the faces of people to get out of the train and be home! Here I was a homeless girl!

The game of the train was about to end, as it was approaching 9pm, and every bone in my body ached from sitting for so long. I had no choice but to take the train to Brixton. I had to head to my corner, and console myself by saying, "Look at the bright side, Pumpi, at least it isn't raining." I thought of calling at Peggy's house, but I said to myself that one night wasn't going to kill me. I walked toward the dark corner, and I don't know why but I burst into tears; just at the thought of what I had brought myself to. Was I justified to torture myself? Or should I just go back and marry any Rasheed or Imran, and be a *chapatti* lady just like them?

It's amazing to know that our choices often lead our lives. Although, we have free will to make those choices, the consequences could be costly. I tried to imagine myself being back there, but amazingly enough, the more I thought about the oppressive living, the more comfortable the concrete ground seemed.

I had a spell of naps that night, but couldn't sleep properly. I was emotionally drained. As dawn approached, I quickly got up and sat on the bench nearby, as if I were waiting for someone! It's sad to acknowledge that when we are victims of circumstance, we tend to hide our wounds, as if we were ashamed of them, or they were our fault! Why do we feel guilty about being victims?

The next day a Chinese boy sat in front of me, in the college. He smiled at me and asked, "Hey! Where the f*** are you from?" I asked him, "What do you mean by f***?" (as I was very eager to learn any new words!)

He then said, "Sorry, man, I shouldn't be speaking like that." He got up from his chair, and offered his hand. "Hello, my name is Lim!" I introduced myself to him, and we have been best friends ever since! I told him the story about my aunt and cousins. He took me to his house and introduced me to his girlfriend, Judith. Lim then showed me the house adjacent to his house, both houses were owned by the same landlord. He showed me a room, which had no glass in the windows, and therefore was vacant. Lim told me his landlord only came once a month, so I could live there rent-free until the landlord caught me. I had no choice whatsoever. I was carrying my suitcase and my rucksack anyway, so I decided to stay there. It was just typical that it suddenly turned into a very chilly night. There was no heater, and no glass in the windows, but being a born optimist I told myself to be grateful that at least it had walls and a ceiling. I could not sleep. The cold chilled me to the bone. My teeth were making music. I clenched the bed sheets and pillow. I cried and begged God to give me a proper shelter.

By now it was 2 or 3am on Friday night/Saturday morning, and I had not had a single hour of sleep. I tried to imagine the heat of Karachi, but the chill in the room was getting into my pores, making my whole body like frozen ice. I heard somebody knocking at the door. I was very worried about who it could be. Two other people shared the house; one of them was named Chong and the other I didn't know.

The tapping on the door got louder. But this time the person on the other side called my name.

"Pumpi, are you up?" the unfamiliar voice asked.

I opened the door and to my amazement it was Lim. He said he worked at a restaurant on Friday nights, and that's why he had come so late. Then he handed me a heater!

"F***ing hell, man, you'll die. I put it out and left it in the kitchen, but Judith forgot to give it you. I knew you couldn't sleep in this cold; there's no f***ing window in this room. Good night, man," he said, and left.

His kind gesture was enough to make my cold night

warm. Great people in our lives are the example of God's presence. I stood there long after he was gone, as it had been so long since anybody was nice to me. Warm tears of happiness rolled down my cheeks. I switched on the heater full blast, but tears kept falling. Every tear prayed for the man with a foul mouth and a golden heart.

It seemed to me that God comes down in the shape of human beings when we deserve to be helped! I stayed there for three weeks, until a room with windows at Morton Road became vacant! I had achieved my first dream, which was to have a place of my own.

I remember when Mr Hughes, the landlord gave me the key: it was like a day of independence for me. I felt I could conquer the world; the feeling was superb! I continued my studies and got a job at a Wimpy Bar, which was quite far from Stratford E15. But I was happy that I was working. My shift was from 6-11pm.

I would get up and go to college, and then head straight to the Wimpy. It was one of those winter nights when Lim told me that it wasn't safe to catch the bus at 11:45pm. The distance from the station to Morton Road was a good forty-five minutes walk. He said I should call him from the station, and he would walk to the station so I could walk back with him (except Friday, of course, as he worked that night). Although I was touched by his sincere offer, I could not take advantage of his kindness.

I felt very strong and happy to have a little place to call home. Lim, my Chinese friend, gave me some plates. I didn't have much money to buy things, but it was still a great feeling to have a place of my own! No father, no brother, and no husband to tell me what to wear or what to do. I started to get good marks in my studies.

It was nearly midnight. The silence of the night was spooky. I was walking back from Wimpy, and had missed the last bus home. My heart was ringing the warning bells. I could sense the terror in the air! It was very chilly, and there was nobody at the bus stop! Or was there? My sixth sense was on the alert, and I could sense danger.

I didn't know what to do! I decided to call Lim. As I approached the phone booth, I spotted a car parked right next to it. Inside I could see only white, shiny teeth. It was like there was a ghost in the car, and then I realized it was a black man sitting in the car smiling at me. The next thing I knew he jumped out of the car, and started running toward me.

Although his car was far away from where I was, the speed of his long legs was like a cheetah leaping for its prey. My mind went numb for a second. I tried to run, but I couldn't find my feet! I had no strength whatsoever! This was the thing I had been dreading all those lonesome nights. This was the event about which Lim had warned me. I looked up to the sky, and asked God to prove to me he was there! I tried to scream, but I had no voice. By this time, the black man was running toward me. Every beat of my heart was faster than a racing car's speedometer. I dropped my bag, and ran for my life. The animal instinct to flee was in me. At one point, I turned back to see how far away he was; fear flowing through my veins like a current. He seemed closer than his shadow. I kept running, and then I reached Stratford Station. A voice inside my head said, "Duck under the ticket collector's counter." I quickly opened the door, and hid myself inside the box. A few minutes went by. However, they seemed like years. I could hear the sound of the man's boots on the cement floor of the station. The sound was getting closer; it was like a grip around my throat.

The floor was cemented and I could hear *shush... shush...* the sound of the boots on the concrete floor. It was quite obvious he was looking for me! My heart was beating faster than the speed of light; my whole body was pouring with sweat. Then I heard "Come on, baby! You know I'll find you! Be a good girl, and I promise I won't hurt you." The moment I heard his voice, I started to weep silently. I was even frightened to cry in case he heard my sobbing, so I put my hand over my mouth. The one thing that surprised me was that he couldn't hear my heart beating! The sound of my heart was *dig...dig...dig...dig.* I couldn't move. I hid in that box until I heard a British Rail type of sound. I felt a little safer.

After a few minutes, I heard footsteps. I peeked out from the glass section of the box, and couldn't see the man that had been chasing me. I felt safe. When I saw a crowd coming out of the train, I emerged from the box sobbing loudly. A couple stopped, and I told them what had happened. I begged them to walk with me, but they insisted I call the police! When you are a foreign student the police are as frightening as that black man on that cold winter's night. I asked another white man and his friend to walk with me, but they also said I should call the police. I thought about calling Lim, but my mind was blank. I could only remember my name, and the fact that I needed to get to Morton Road. I couldn't even remember Lim's phone number.

Suddenly, I saw a white man walking with a black man toward the exit. I ran to them.

"Please help me, I was chased by a man. Could you please walk with me to…?"

I screamed for help. My whole body was shaking with terror. I didn't know whether that man was still outside the station or not. I didn't have money for a cab. I was in a terrible situation. The white man was very sympathetic.

"Where do you live?" he asked.

I wanted to say Morton Road, but my lips were shaking terribly, and they couldn't understand me. They asked me to sit down and relax. The white man gave me his bottle of water. It felt like heaven to have a drop of water. I then managed to say Morton Road. The white man said it was out of their way. The black man folded the newspaper into his other arm and said, "It's okay, I'll walk wit' you, man."

"But it's really far from where you live. As a matter of fact it's in the opposite direction," the white man said.

I wasn't sure whether to trust that black man or not after my bitter experience with the other black man. But I realized I had little choice, so I decided to walk with him. I was frightfully aware of the repercussions of the journey. Every bush I saw made me think of how vulnerable I was, although I knew he was not the same man that had chased me. After a long walk, which seemed longer than the walk of life itself, I saw Morton Road. My door was very near, and yet so far!

He walked me all the way to the little red gate. My legs

were still shaking with terror. I had never felt like that in my entire life. I tried to put the key into the lock, but my hands were shaking violently. I noticed the black man walking toward me. He took the key from my hand and opened the door. I was still speechless, waiting to be assaulted by him.

"Good night, sister," he said, and then walked away!

At that moment I realized he was a genuine person. The only thing that frightened me was his colour, which was a result of my own ignorance. I saw his back and realized how ungrateful I had been. I didn't even thank him!

I shouted, "Excuse me." He stopped in his tracks, as if transfixed. Then I ran to him.

"Thank you seems like a small word for your kindness. I really thought you would be like the other black man," I said to him.

"All black men are not rapists and murderers," he replied pitifully. I felt deeply ashamed.

"Thank you. May you live all the days of your life. God bless you!" I said to him, and gave him a warm hug.

Any port in a storm

When I arrived in England I was amazed to see there were no children on the streets of London, while in my country children scrounged food from the rubbish of the street, and begged for money to feed themselves and their young siblings. If they were fortunate enough to go to school, they had to sit under the streetlights in the evening to do their homework, as they had no electricity in their homes. But in Britain, the sea of knowledge was open for all. In England, the passion for learning amongst people, regardless of their age, was fascinating to me. This was the place where women were given a sense of individuality; they were competing side by side with men. It was a breath of fresh air to see that women were not left at home to keep the bed and meal warm for their spouses. I fell in love with England.

In 1986, after being in the country for about three months, I found an admirer. An old friend of my flatmate, Lim, Richard was a very understanding and caring man.

Although he was more than ten years older than me, he said he was madly in love with me, and had a great respect for my ambitious outlook on life. Being brought up in an Islamic culture, there was never an opportunity for a man to tell me he liked me. I was never told that my views had any meaning, so it was very exciting for me to hear all that from an Englishman.

The sense of oblivion turned into recognition. I was alive like a man in my country. I now had a say in life's major decisions! There was a girl called Pumpi, not the eldest daughter of Mr Hameed, who was ready for slaughter in the name of tradition. I was ecstatic to know that a young Muslim girl had been discovered, and was able to snatch a chance to live the way she wanted to live!

I was exuberant on my wedding day. I didn't have many friends at that time, but nevertheless my college teacher, John, and his girlfriend were kind enough to be there for us. I was elated by the opportunity to make one of life's major decisions! It was the acceptance of my physical and mental being that I could make a decision. Whether it was the right or wrong one only time would tell!

What If?

It didn't take that long before I realized my happiness was transitory. In one night it all changed! Richard brought a young guy home with him. He told me James was an old friend of his from Leeds, and that since he didn't have any place to stay in London, he would be staying with us for three nights. Since we lived in a bed-sit, I assumed James would sleep in the kitchen, but to my amazement Richard insisted he sleep in our bedroom.

I felt there was something fishy going on. Just before dinner, Richard and James were whispering and counting money at the kitchen table. I couldn't find out what they were up to. Every woman has the gift of noticing the look in a man's eyes, and I was no different. The look in James's eyes made me feel very uncomfortable. A man does not look at his friend's wife the way he was looking at me.

At about 11:30pm, I left Richard and James in the kitchen, and went to bed. About an hour later, I was awoken by the sound of laughter and a strong smell of aftershave very close to my face. I switched on the light. The next thing I knew James was on our bed, completely naked, trying to undress me. I was horrified. I screamed and jumped out of bed. Even more saddening to me than James's animalistic behaviour was the fact that Richard sat nearby observing it all.

I screamed with the pain of humiliation and disgust. James grabbed me by the shoulders, and pushed me onto the bed. Then he tried to grab me. I tried to run away from him, but he kept pushing me onto the bed. Richard kept laughing. I screamed at him, and eventually managed to pull my naked body out of the nightie. I then ran to the kitchen, and stayed there for the rest of the night. I was numbed by Richard's behaviour. Until then Richard and I were having a peaceful life. Suddenly this little castle of hope simply crumbled before my very eyes. I had never seen that side of Richard. It was a very self-doubting moment for me. Richard was not a drinker so no one could say his actions were caused by alcohol. Therefore it was very hurtful for me, and I doubted whether I would ever be able to trust him or anyone again. All night tears rolled down my cheeks, and then I reached a point where on the surface there were no tears, but inside the weeping continued, washing away any trace of love or trust.

My ignorance led me to believe there was nothing I could have done to stop the attempted rape. In fact I was not even aware that that was what the act was called. In the kitchen I found the linen basket. I put on as many clothes as I could, and waited for the morning.

In the morning, Richard and James were gone. They didn't even come to the kitchen for their morning coffee. I went to the bedroom; apart from the strong smell of aftershave, there was nothing to suggest that an attempted rape had occurred the previous night. I kept asking myself questions. Did it really happen? Could Richard be such a bastard? I couldn't find my ripped nightie to prove to myself that it had. Then I saw the scratches on my arms, which made me believe that love is like a cigarette; it starts with a spark, and ends with ashes! I was too depressed to face anyone, so I didn't go to work that day.

It was about eight o'clock that evening when Richard came home, alone. He tried to explain to me that he owed

James £95, and that it had been James's idea as he didn't have the money to repay him. He was still smiling about it.

I was revolted by Richard's explanation. For the first time in my entire life, I was at a loss for words. I was boiling inside, but outside I was frozen.

Marriage is like having a beautiful dream. Once you are woken up, you can never go back to the same dream again. It can only stay in your memory. — APM

CHAPTER FOUR

Love, deceit and betrayal

After divorcing Richard, I decided to concentrate on my career and nothing else. Soon, from being a cleaner in St Thomas's Hospital, I had become a manageress of an Indian restaurant called Chutneys. I was delighted to work 11 hours a day, and meeting new people every day. Life has brought me comfort and luxury at my foot.

I bought lots of clothes, as this was the first time since I arrived in London, that I had any money. I always love the harmony of colours. I had a matching bra to matching hair clip. It was amazing to see that money can't buy happiness however, it can sure makes you buy things that in turn make you happy. I was very fortunate to have a flat in Hampstead, beautiful clothes, lots of money in the bank. There were times I used to wake up and check my bank statement and open my wardrobe to reassure that I am not a homeless lonely girl in London any more.

However, my views about women's liberation were soon discovered by the Muslim management which caused a great friction and eventually I resigned from the restaurant. As I had a great faith in myself, I knew that I would find a decent job soon. In 1988 I became the Area Manageress of 12 hotels in Victoria, London. And I bought a flat in Frognal, Hampstead, London.

It was a great time of my life, as I could afford to buy what ever I wanted to buy.

My life was too busy working and shopping for books and clothes. Although I was still in my twenties and single, I did not feel the need to have a boy friend.

"We make our fortunes and we call them fate." – DISRAELI

In July 1988, in Frognal, Hampstead, the glorious sun was shining at its peak. I was walking very slowly, as my four-inch heels were slowing me down. All of a sudden, the vein of sun ruptured, and rain started to embrace every part of Hampstead. The compulsive rain made my white silk blouse stick to my breasts. As I had no umbrella, I soon became drenched. Cars passed by slowly. Then all of a sudden, a green car stopped, and a very charming young man got out.

"Oh my God, you are soaking wet! You have a f***ing beautiful face. Jesus Christ, you are so beautiful. I bet it's original, not a bottle tan," he said.

"How can you tell?" I asked, intrigued.

"It would have been washed away by now by the rain," he laughed.

He then offered his hand and said, "Hi, I'm Carl."

I shook his hand. "Hello, I'm Pumpi," I replied.

"Pompeii!" he exclaimed. "I thought you were Italian."

"No, I am Pak-made, with an Italian package," I responded.

"Could I have the pleasure of dropping you where you want to go?" he asked.

At first I found it very difficult to understand his thick, Irish brogue. But after he repeated it with great patience, I understood the offer and accepted. However, I was totally unaware that this was to become the most expensive ride of my life. I later became his wife – and the victim of his physical and mental abuse – for five very long years.

Carl had an extremely charming, as well as convincing, personality. He could convince the Pope to buy a condom from him! He convinced me that he was the kindest person in the world. His love for me was unquestionable. He was overprotective; it was later on that I realized that it was called chronic possessiveness.

But after my experience with Richard, I loved his over-protectiveness. I suppose this is the problem with many people when they start a new relationship; they tend to compare, rather than judging each person on their own merit. Carl's encouraging and gentlemanly ways eventually won my heart. Carl put me on a pedestal so high that I was unable to see how low he was.

Carl saw me as a beautiful woman, he could not stop praising me. I was flattered and very excited, as all through my childhood I had been told I was ugly and too dark. My father displayed his dislike toward me on several occasions. He used to buy beautiful jewellery for my younger sister, but not for me. I remember asking him once why he didn't buy any earrings and bangles for me. I still remember his harsh reply.

"Seemi has got a dolly face; just go and look at your face, you have an ugly face and an evil tongue."

I was extremely degraded. I ran upstairs to my bedroom, but felt too desolate to look at my face. Parents often forget they are the cause of our existence. If we are ugly, they are ugly. In fact, in my life I still have not found a single child who is ugly. I believe innocence itself is beautiful, and every child possesses that beauty. When we say a child is ugly, we see our own ugliness in them.

Despite Carl's loving affection in the beginning, I had a very strong gut feeling telling me to keep my distance from this man, but I put those feelings down to a sign of insecurity! Carl was a very charming and convincing man. He managed to persuade me that his love for me was unconditional. And his violence toward me was due to lack of security, once we are married Carl said he would feel more secure and assured me that violence would be stopped. And after living with him, in a volatile situation, on May 5th 1990, I got married for the third time! A hat trick! My marriage record was a disgrace for a Syed family. It seemed as if I was like a serial killer, but instead of killing people, I was on a 'marriage spree'.

PRESENCE OF AN ABSENTEE?

The week Carl and I met, he told me he wanted me to meet his family in Ireland. We travelled to Mullingar, Ireland, where he asked me to promise in front of his twin brother that I would never leave him. He then took me to a cemetery, and showed me the final resting place of his twin brother, Michael Samuel Moore, who had died in a car accident, ten days before Christmas 1986.

In the Muslim culture, girls do not visit cemeteries; therefore it was the first time I had been in a graveyard. I was quite numbed. Carl asked me to hold my hand on Michael's headstone, and promise him I would never leave Carl. The eerie feeling was overpowered by the prominent sense of assurance of non-assuring life itself. The moment I touched the headstone, I felt a very strong energy around me. I felt somebody was there, listening to every word I said. I looked at Carl for affirmation. But he was kneeling by the grave-side, sobbing bitterly. After a while we left the resting place. Even today, life itself, and that feeling of somebody being with me, stays with me! That was the first time I had had such a strange experience. I thought it was due to my lack of experience at the cemetery. But to my surprise, it became a lifelong companionship with someone I had never ever met. Even when Carl's abusive behaviour became out of control and there were many nights when I desperately wanted to leave him, there was a strange energy around me telling me not to break my promise. I strongly believed it was Michael's spirit that was around me. I told a few of my friends about this spiritual experience, but they didn't believe me. Nevertheless, it continued for most of the time I was with Carl.

Many years later, in 1999, just after my graduation from law school, I visited a psychic, whose number I had obtained after overhearing a group of women at a party. I was unaware that she was also a medium. While sitting in her room, she sensed a spiritual presence around us. The flickering of candles was imminent. She was quiet for a moment, and then stared at me. "This spirit came for you, they passed away with an impact," she explained. She told me his name was Michael, and that he had passed away in a car accident at a very young age. "He is congratulating you on something, and thanking you for something as well," she added. "It is as if you made an agreement with him, a kind of promise; he's saying it's fine, you can move forward." The psychic then asked me, "Have you got a child, a son? Did you honour him with the late Michael's name?"

My lips were sealed like glue to paper. I nodded my head. She said, "He is thanking you for that."

I was blown away by her revelations. After a very long time my spiritual fears were finally realized. All that time when I had told Carl and my friends about Michael's spiritual presence in my life, no one had believed me. Nevertheless, here I was with a total stranger who had confirmed my fears. I founded it truly amazing, and therapeutic, that I had such a deep spiritual connection with a man I had never physically met.

The art of isolation

I always had many friends, but Carl's attitude made me lose my friends one by one. Most of these violent men know exactly how to gain trust and how to isolate their victims. The art of isolation is hypnotic. The vital part of the abuser's control over the victim is to make sure that the victim has nobody to turn to. Paradoxically the process of eliminating the victim's friends is often done by the victim, without them acknowledging the implications. By the time the victim realizes the magnitude of the problem, they are desperately lonely. It is the acute loneliness that is enough to turn strength into weakness, logic into disproportion, and sane into insane.

Carl's insecurity made him a very possessive and jealous man. He never had friends, only drinking partners. On the contrary, I had many friends, from all over the world. On my wedding day somebody commented that "it looks like a UN function, rather than a wedding ceremony". But I still managed to lose some of my good friends.

Carl was spending too much money on beer and on gambling machines. The time came when he could not even pay the telephone bill. Carl's work depended on the phone calls, as he was a self-employed handyman. I had a newborn baby, therefore, I decided to stay at home with the baby till he was two or three. We asked one of my friends, Tony, if we could use his phone number on the advertisements and as always, my friends were there to support me. After about three or four weeks my husband told me that he was not getting any phone calls because Tony (whose phone we were using) was not passing on the messages, instead he was stealing the jobs himself. It sounded plausible because Tony was doing the same kind of work, but that was totally out of character. I was under the spell of my hypnotist. I had to see what I was shown. I believed every word that Carl said. And spoilt my good, honest friendship with Tony.

My whole being was like a puppet on the string. I had no power of thinking. I could not see for myself. One day he told me about one of my very close Iranian friends. She had been calling him at his work and asking him to go out with her. Then one day he told me that she turned up at work. I could not believe him at first, or anything. Carl told me he did not want her to come and see me, as she was a low character girl. As far as I was concerned, Carl could not be wrong. I stop replying to her phone calls, and eventually the friendship faded away. I had no one who could tell me that 'friends are forever, do not compromise your friends'. By the time I noticed that Carl had made me an island: it was too late to do anything.

CHAPTER FIVE

DOMESTIC VIOLENCE
No one can make you feel inferior, without your own consent. – ELEANOR ROOSEVELT

THE EXTENSIVE EXPERIENCES of my life vary from being the victim of a traditionally arranged Asian marriage to my departure from my home country and subsequent marriages. However, was male domination unique to the Islamic world? I soon learnt otherwise!

Domestic violence is not unusual. It takes place everywhere, from the villages of India to the trendy apartments in New York City. Each case is unique in its own way, as it tells a different story. Yet no matter the location, each has a certain key element in common: violence suffered by an innocent individual, caused by a demented loved one. A violent relationship does not start suddenly. It is like a cancer, spreading slowly, but surely. Often by the time one discovers the disease, it has spread all over the body and one has no time to recover. Therefore it is crucial that once one sees the symptoms, one should seek the treatment. These violent men can be quite ingenious in their own wicked ways, in order to restrain their victims. The perpetrator often enters one's life as a friend, and the first target is to gain one's trust. Then dependency follows.

When I met Carl, I had a thriving business in Victoria. I had many people working for me. Nevertheless, little by little Carl managed to persuade me that my employees were dishonest. I believed him, because my trust in him was like a nun to Christ. I had friends, but one by one, I lost most of them.

"Is love like a cigarette, starting with a spark and ending with ashes?"

It was the end of May 1990, about 7am. We had been married for only three weeks. I was in a deep sleep, when suddenly I felt somebody pulling my hair. The next thing, I noticed I was being dragged along the floor by Carl. I tried to pull my head away, but his grip was very strong. I tried opening my eyes, as wide as I could. At that time I could only believe I was having a nightmare. Then I realized that it was no bad dream. Carl then yanked my hair so that I was forced to stand up. I felt like a puppet. I was half-asleep, but the severity of the pain woke me from my peaceful slumbers.

My abuser then said, "Make some breakfast for me. This is not your father's house, and there aren't any servants here." I resented his demand. I craved for the courage to kick him out of the flat. But then I realized that If I could not even pull my hair away from him, what chance was there that I would have the strength to fight with him, or even run away from him? From the depth of my heart, I prayed that he would die. I thought it better not to argue. As they say "while in water don't argue with the crocodile". I looked at the semi-bright side that, if I made the breakfast, at least he would go to work and I would be safe. Amidst the hullabaloo a milk bottle fell to the floor, shattered into pieces, and splashed liquid all around. I was like a frightened child who knew that his brutal mother would beat the hell out of him. I took the cloth, and sat on the floor to wipe away the mess.

My petite hands were spread over the cleaning material, ready to get down to work, when suddenly I saw two safety boots in front of me. Slowly I turned to look up. His anger was palpable. I screamed with pain as he put both boots on my hands and squashed my fingers. Then he grabbed my hair and rubbed my face on the floor, using it like some instrument to wipe away the spilt milk. I felt degraded. My self-esteem was non-existent. It was as if I had somehow cheated or betrayed myself, by allowing him to treat me in the manner that he just did. The sense of humiliation was indescribable. Carl kept shouting at me, "You f***ing bitch, how I am suppose to have my f***ing coffee?" He kept rubbing and bashing my face on the floor. I was weeping with tears quietly, but inside my heart I was screaming with anger. That was the morning I had to believe in hell and heaven. Why do people say we reach heaven and hell after death? I believe we face both on earth. What we end up with is the result of our actions in a previous life.

The echoes of my brutal mother were coming back to me, "That's what you deserve, Pumpi – you asked for it." In my mind I was shouting, " Stop! Stop before I kill you." Deep down I knew my only fault was to allow them to treat me in the manner they did. My heart was questioning God. Do I really deserve this? Was I to blame?

I started to get ready to go to work. I very much wanted to disappear and not come back. But I could not rid myself of the fear that Carl might find me. And if he did, I thought, he would definitely kill me. The very thought was enough to send shivers running down my spine. Therefore, I can easily sympathize with women who find themselves in a similar predicament, and face the same fear. Although Carl was a perfect gentleman when I met him. It was terribly hard for me to imagine how a person could have changed so much in such a short time? Looking back, I realise that there were times when I thought that he might be the same person he later proved to be. But then I would stop, and chide myself for apparently misjudging him.

These violent people are extremely dangerous, because they can disguise themselves. They are not like a cigarette packet that comes with the government health warning!

Over- and underestimation factors

We often don't credit ourselves for the potential we possess. One of the problems I faced was the feeling that I deserved whatever brutal treatment I was getting. I would like to call this 'underestimating my self-worth'. Although I acknowledged that what Carl was doing was wrong, I always reassured myself that he was a strong person, so he would change! I was overestimating his potential.

The home is the chief school of human virtues.
– William Ellery Channing

The day went by and the evening fell. Carl came home with a bunch of red roses, acting as if nothing had happened in the morning. He was as sweet as a pea. I tried very hard to bring to his attention the incident that morning, and his cruel behaviour. But he kept changing the topic. Finding him in a far better mood, I plucked up my courage and told him, "I want you to control your temper, otherwise sooner or later you will lose me."

Carl was very happy to listen to every word I was saying. He put his head on my lap, and said "I love you so much, so never judge my love by how I treat you in anger, and I only get angry because you make me angry." I said to him: "I still can't believe you can treat me like dirt." He then tried to convince me that it was all my fault.

After dinner, he made a phone call to his father. I was horrified to hear the joy with which he related each violent act as he described that day's incidents. I was shocked to hear the lack of remorse, even the sense of pride, in his voice. Carl was describing in detail how he woke me up, and how many times he pushed my face against the floor. It was terrifying to hear Carl's conversation with his father. I was petrified at the idea of bringing up a child in such a violent atmosphere. I suppose a father who could listen and appreciate such aggressive behaviour with such equanimity might equally teach his son to act in that manner!

Late evening I called my father-in-law and expressed my anger at Carl's behaviour. I was horrified to hear his pride, when he quoted the Bible in his reply.

EPHESIANS 5:22-33

'Wives, submit yourselves unto your own husbands, as unto the Lord.'

I could not believe that after travelling from East to West, the basis of oppression of women was exactly the same, in the name of religion!

LOVE IS BLIND – AS WELL AS DEAF! (APM)

Like most violent men, Carl was also a control freak. His violence varied from a punch on my face, to strangling me during the night. The strange factor of the relationship was his powerful ability to convince me that every time he beat me up, was 'my fault'. It was easy for me to accept, as it was the same 'punch line' from my mother, "See Pumpi what you make me do to you". Although most of his fury was fuelled by alcohol; however, he managed to convince me that he only drank because I gave him hell at home. Therefore, he needed to go out and relax with a few pints of beer.

Love is blind: we can look, but not see. Love camouflages our vision. Others can see what is happening to us, but we can't see for ourselves. On the other hand, love is deaf, too. When we are in love, we only hear, not listen! We have selective listening while in love. Vikky was a very kind friend of mine, for a long time she did not see my bruises. I wanted to tell her but there were two factors which was stopping me to reveal the truth. I knew she loved me too much it would hurt her tremendously, plus I was ashamed or I suppose to some extent guilty, because deep down I was convinced by Carl, that his violent behaviour was not his fault but mine, therefore how could I say to anyone that he was doing anything wrong. However, one day Vikky received some dresses from the Philippines, her home country. She called me over to her place, which was not far. Carl was at work. It was great fun to try different dresses. As I was changing into a beautiful floral summer dress from my long sleeve dress, Vikky's face suddenly looked sad. I did not notice that she was facing my back, which normally had marks, sometimes fresh bruises, sometimes old ones. She walked towards me and asked me what it was. I was frozen. Vikky's eyes filled with tears and horror. I felt as if those eyes would pop out of their sockets. She started screaming at me. "How could you let this happen to you Pumpi?" She kept crying and screaming at me. She did not even ask where I got those marks. Well I suppose my silence was more explicit than words.

It does not matter how many friends or professionals may warn us that we are embarking on a road to disaster. We cannot understand what they are saying, because we are unable to listen.

Carl was now working as a fitter and earning good money. We were still living in Hampstead. Carl spent most of his money on gambling and beer. The only time he would spend money on anything in the house was when parents were coming over from Ireland. It was one of those weekends when Carl's parents were planning to stay with us. Carl decorated the place at some cost, and then gave me £10 to buy a teapot. I went to a small shop to purchase the item. The shopkeeper put the teapot into a carrier bag, and after I paid her, I began walking back towards the bus stop. Unfortunately, my hand hit a pole by accident, and I heard a sudden crack. Opening the bag, I discovered that the teapot had cracked into pieces. I was petrified. The horror of Carl beating me again was freezing my blood. I felt my veins run dry. I went back to the shop and burst into tears. The lovely English woman who sold the teapot to me a while ago was still there. She asked me if I was alright. I asked her if she could replace the teapot. She was right to say no, because she had shown me the teapot before putting it into the bag, and it was in one piece! I just knew how much I would be punched and kicked by the psychopath. I was highly embarrassed to ask her, but I had no choice. I just wanted to hide some place. I did not have money to replace the teapot.

What if?

The woman led me over to one side, and asked me what was the matter. I told her about my husband's fury whenever I made a mistake. I told her about a previous incident when I had washed his white jumper with coloured clothes, and it was ruined; and how on another occasion he had brutally beaten me with a belt. I explained to her how I just could not afford to tell Carl the truth, that it was my fault the teapot was broken. I was crying bitterly by this stage. The woman was very kind. She gave me a glass of water, and told me that I should leave a man like him. She also agreed to replace the teapot. Although, she was quite right to say I should not stay with a man like him, but it was not that easy. These violent men have a grip on your throat, even when they are miles away from you.

I came home and cried all night. What have I made of myself, I asked? In the past I used to handle 30 to 40 male staff, and dealt with aggressive clients. So why couldn't I handle this man? I kept probing myself for the answers. What was the difference between them and Carl? Yet the answer was just there, staring me in the face! I was not in love with any of those other men. It is the negative power of love that makes us surrender our willpower. At first we enjoy losing that power, and we let the love overpower us. But at times, this power can be lethal. Just before 7pm, I decided that I would stand up for my rights. Nevertheless, the thought of facing him, his piercing eyes on my face, could make me sweat with fear. And that was when he was not even there. How then could I face up to him in person?

I felt an awful, devastating sense of imprisonment. It was weirder still, because you feel like you are in jail, while all the doors and windows remain open! The fear of isolation alone was enough to suffocate me.

It was my childhood experience that was pushing me to leave the hostile marriage. I have to admit that my married life was worse than my parents' married life, as we had never seen our father ever hitting our mother. I was only married for seven weeks, and I was thinking of leaving my husband. It was a heart-breaking decision. I was feeling torn apart. One part of my brain was saying that was the right decision, the other half was telling me that Carl will cut you into pieces. I wanted somebody to wave a magic wand over Carl, so that he would treat me with respect. I had given up on love, even to treat me decently would be fine for me to stay in the marriage.

I was afraid that I could not face myself with three failed marriages. The flood of questions kept coming to my mind. Do I not take marriage seriously? What man will marry a woman who has left three husbands? Are failures actually successes? Then I thought that at the end of the day we all sleep on our own pillow. It is that pillow that absorbs our tears when love turns you into bruises, when trust is sold for money. The thought 'what will people say?' came to my mind. But my will power did not allow me to hide behind the shadows of people's opinion. In my opinion, if somebody is shallow enough to judge you without knowing you, then they themselves aren't worth knowing. I was entangled with all these harsh thoughts when I saw a black BMW car stop in front of our flat in Frognal Mansions. I had mixed emotions. Although I was the one who asked my friend Amanda's help in my rescue, when she arrived with her boy friend Dave, I was unable to make any decisions at that time. I did want to leave Carl, but I could not do it on my own. He had drained all my strength. This was my golden opportunity, as one of my good friends was arriving to take me away from this cruel man.

Amanda walked towards me and hugged me. I was crying with severe pain, as if Carl had died. But I suppose he had died a long time ago. It was I who was in denial all this time. Dave told us that we should not waste any crucial moments.

I then took a last look at Frognal Mansions. It was horrifying to acknowledge that, just less than two months ago, I was stepping down from those long stairs, in my wedding gown! I remember how thrilled I had been that day. The stream of tears I shed was like British rain – totally non-stop. Dave put the suitcase in the boot and closed it. We were there for about four to five minutes at the most, when I spotted Carl's van pulling into Frognal Mansions. My whole body started to shake. Carl never came home that early, and it was only quarter to five. He usually returned at about 7 or 7:30pm. Moreover, Amanda, Dave and myself had arranged our operation especially for Friday, because on pay day Carl used to go to the pub and seldom returned before 9 or 10pm. All three of us were baffled. Dave said quickly: "Just tell him we were in the area and just popped in for tea." That was so un-English, but we had no other option. Carl came towards us with his bright smile. He greeted all of us.

"We were just going," Dave announced. "We were in the Futon shop and we decided to come around and give you guys a surprise visit," Amanda added. "How did you know that Pumpi was off? Are you psychic or something?" Carl asked with deep suspicion in his voice. I knew in his words he was saying, "What the f… is going on?"

Dave quickly interrupted "We called in the morning and she answered – simple." He then asked Carl if he would like to join us all for a drink out somewhere. Carl's facial expression was enough to convince me that my master plan had flown out of the window.

My heart was sinking. Carl's refusal to go to the pub was a sign of major disaster. Surely the world had to be in turmoil, the day an Irish man refuses to go to a pub! I could sense the tension in the atmosphere. Then I felt a sense of defeat.

My suitcase was still in Dave's car, and the absence of my toothbrush would be the first thing Carl would notice. I was petrified for that moment. I wished that I could be in the boot of the car, in place of the suitcase. My friend and her boyfriend had taken time off to help me, for my sake. Nevertheless we just missed out by two or three minutes! I wanted to open my mouth and shout at God, "Why?"

"So, do you want to come with us to the pub?" Amanda then asked me. Before I could say anything, Carl said, "Pumpi does not drink, you should know that. Besides, I am really hungry. Darling, what is for dinner?" His eyes cut me, right through my body, shredding me into little pieces. I just held my tears and looked at Amanda and Dave. My silent screams were echoing the atmosphere. By this time Carl was tapping his keys on the van, making a *tic, tic* sound. For me, it was like somebody inside myself, telling me that time was running out! Run…run…run…!

The moment was stationary. The air felt static.

"OK, better be going to have a shower. Are you guys coming in for tea?" Carl suggested. "No, in fact we just had tea with Pumpi, so we're just leaving," Amanda explained. Dave looked angry and confused.

"I think, Pumpi, you should come for a drink," he then said. Dave's assertive way made Carl more suspicious. Carl looked at me. I was like a mouse, trapped in a cage. After seeing the miserable and helpless look, Dave calmly said, "Well, it's up to you!" Yet somebody inside myself was screaming that it was not up to me! In fact, if it was, then I would have left him the first day he slapped me across my face.

I wanted to move towards the BMW, but my feet felt heavier than mountains. I was devastated to see my friends leave without me. There are times in one's life when only the person who is in a particular situation can understand the gravity of the moment.

I walked a mile with sorrow, Never a word said she,
But, oh! The things I learnt from her,
when sorrow walked with me. – ROBERT BROWNING

Dave turned the car around. I followed it with my eyes, feeling as if somebody had snatched a golden key from my hand. There was such a deep pain in my heart. I sighed heavily. All I could do was cry in silence. As Carl and I entered the apartment at Frognal Mansions, I went inside quickly and hid the note on the fridge. I knew Carl had suspected that some plan was afoot, so I was terrified of the likely repercussions. I went to the kitchen to make coffee for Carl. As I was taking out the cup, he walked in and peered into the basin. At first I did not know what he was looking at, and why he seemed stunned. Suddenly he turned to me, and his big strong hand just slapped me across the face. "Don't think that you can make me look a fool!" he yelled. He then nailed me against the wall, pushing my face against his. He got hold of my chin, and jerked it up with his fist. His thumb was pressing on my vocal chords. I felt severe pain around my neck. Nevertheless, there was nothing I could have done to ease the sensation. Carl kept saying to me that there was no cup in the basin, nobody was here, so what was going on? Then came another slap on my face. When I tried to protect myself with my hands, he did exactly what my mother used to do, and said: "Don't try to hide. The more you hide the more you get, Pumpi." I was amazed by the sheer fact that these violent people – separated by time, culture and continents – even chose the very same sentences. Then I managed to escape, though I did not get very far. I ran to the toilet and locked myself in. I was afraid of what Carl was going to do to. Perhaps he might even kill me. Carl started to slam the door, banging it repeatedly. We were living in Hampstead, a very peaceful area of London. The knocking was getting louder and louder – and with each bang I felt I was growing smaller. Suddenly, the door's lock broke, shattered by the sheer force of Carl's boots. I felt the blood had vanished from my body. I was desperately hoping that the noise would alert somebody and they would call the police! But I suppose everybody was thinking, 'some body else would call the police'. Of course, nobody did!

The door flew open. I felt as if my heart had seized. All I could see in front of me was a six-foot tall angry Irishman. His usually big beautiful eyes were now bloodshot. His fists were clenched, and his teeth were tightly closed. I was sitting in the corner, like a cat terrified of its cruel master. My throat was dry with fear. I could not believe my bad luck. I had the golden opportunity to escape, but I missed it by minutes. Devastation was a very soft word to describe those boiling emotions.

Carl was moving towards me very slowly, and the toilet was extremely small. It seemed like a lifetime – or like someone awaiting their final retribution.

"Why did you guys lie to me? Amanda said she had tea with you! I knew there was something else going on! All the cups are washed and dry! Tell me what were you thinking to do with them?" Carl shouted at me with fierce anger.

I had literally no voice in my throat to explain anything. He grabbed hold of my hand brought me to the bedroom, and then pushed me to the bed and sat on my chest. I could barely breathe. My breasts were aching with pain. He kept asking me to tell him what I was doing with them? Every question was accompanied by a punch on my breasts. I wondered why God makes violent people so physically strong? But I could not get an answer back from God, as it must have been His day off! Carl then snatched at my expensive perfumes, and sprayed them on my hair. He knew I loved my long hair. One after the other, he wasted my perfumes and damaged my hair.

The smell of the mixture of perfumes was strange. However, I was still grateful to him, that at least it was not as painful as I was expecting. It is appalling yet true that in domestic violence the victim gets immune to the abuse, if it persists long enough. Although the victim does not lose the ability to feel pain, nevertheless, to some extent, she begins to lose self-respect along the line. And when she experiences less severe abuse than usual, she feels grateful to her abuser for diminished cruelty on that particular occasion.

I thought that Carl had gone for the night. But before long he returned, this time with a rope in his hand. I was tired of even living at that time. I was not sure what he was going to do. He came close to me and tied my hands and legs together. I was feeling so low that death seemed more inviting than life itself. I was not even worried at that time, as my level of thinking had sunk to its lowest point. I was like a person in a coma. I had no power or energy left in me. He then said, "Tell me, were you planning to run away, or have group sex with them?" I was amazed at his imagination. But I really had no strength to say a word. Then he just left. I was still happy that I had not received the beatings that I normally did. I was left in the small toilet with my hands and legs bound together. My wristwatch was intact, and I had my wedding ring and the engagement ring on my finger. I kept staring at them. So I remained for five hours, my body growing as numb as my mind felt.

I waited for a very long time, but Carl did not come back, as it was his payday and he had to go out for fruit machines and boozing. Although I was inside the bathroom I could not actually use the toilet. Suddenly I wet myself without warning. I felt like the lowest of the low. By now it was morning, and the room was smelling with my wee. I was worse than an animal. Even a cat gets a chance to hide her pee with sand. My eyes were dry, for I could not shed any tears over my plight. I knew my anger was reaching the stage where killing the abuser was the ultimate retaliation.

The next day I heard the door opening. I was exhausted with the sheer torture of the past twelve hours. The smell in the toilet was making me puke. Carl came to the room and couldn't stop laughing at me. At first he put the hand over his face then he said "Oh! my God! You have peed. My father would love to hear this one." He then added, "Baby, next time daddy will put a nappy on you." He undid the knots on my feet and hands. I was physically and emotionally exhausted. I soaked myself in the bath.

I strongly believe that if I had had self-respect in my childhood, it would have been much easier for me to stand up for myself sooner. There are many types of crimes, but not loving yourself, and then projecting your lack of self-worth onto one's children could be the biggest crime of all. The major problem is that most children are the by-product of sex, rather than the product of lovemaking. Therefore they are not loved as much as they should be.

What surprises me is the attitude of most people. They spend too much time buying property or a new car. They also plan their holidays in advance, yet when it comes to bringing human beings into this world, most people don't think for a second. We see posters saying, "A dog is not for Christmas, it's for life." What about kids? People don't realize the importance of their duty as parents. Sex is a serious business, with great consequences. Having a child is not like a car that you can trade in, the moment you get bored. It is not a holiday on which you can claim insurance if it goes wrong. This is a serious business, with serious consequences.

Another attempt to escape

I plucked up the courage one more time to run away from my violent husband.

I met up with my friend Nina. After a long discussion with her, we decided that the only way I could escape the mental and physical torture was to leave Carl, for good. The only way I could achieve that would be by not returning home one evening from work. But the fear of being caught was petrifying and furthermore, he used to pick me up from my work. However, I was determined. So I then decided that I would go to Nina's flat rather than to work. She agreed. The day I had been waiting for came on a hot summer's day. It was hard to find Nina among millions of unfamiliar faces at the station. We eventually met at Tottenham Court Road Station. We then started walking ever faster as the time went by, like two fugitives! I felt worried and frightened, however Nina lived in East London, far away from Carl.

The clock struck six o'clock, as my nerves started to rise. I felt as if they were going to bust out of my temple. My friend was trying to calm me down, but it did not work, I was as frightened as ever. I did not tell anybody, except one of my Asian friends, Shahid, about my escape route. I knew Shahid long before I met Carl, and he treated me like a sister. I had every reason to trust him.

At 10pm, the same evening, I called Shahid to find out how angry Carl was. However, Shahid tried to convince me that I was wrong to leave Carl. At first I could not believe what he was saying as he was one of the friends who had seen my bruises. He told me that I was like a sister to him; this was the same advice he would have given to his sister in the same dilemma. I could see his Muslim upbringing was undermining his logic. He told me that what Carl had done was wrong, but you were to stay in a marriage. He then said, "Are you going to make a record of some kind? For God's sake, he is your husband. He does have every right to keep you in control."

Shahid sounded like a typical Muslim brother, who believes that a married woman's place is her husband's house, and after that the cemetery. No place in between.

The main problem with most Asian Muslim men is their hypocritical way of living. On one hand, living in Britain, they would like to consider themselves as British. They fight to be recognized as British. They pretend to be Westernised, by drinking and playing golf, but when it comes to mentality – Asian men's thinking – they can't match the civilised ways and fairness of most Western men.

I told Shahid to inform Carl that I had left my job, and was calling from Scotland. I was still too frightened to go to work, just in case Carl turned up!

I spent a sleepless night at Nina's flat. Shahid called me the next day, to see how I was. I was absolutely depressed and frightened, therefore, he asked me to meet up. I was stupid enough to give him Nina's address! Shahid arrived at Nina's door with a pizza. He stayed for a long time. All the time he tried to convince me to go back to Carl. I had made my mind up and I was prepared to fight on. Shahid left late that night with the promise not to let Carl know, where I was.

Next day Nina went to work. I was still scared for my life. It was about 11am, when the doorbell rang the blood in my body froze. But soon a young man's voice said, "Parcel delivery!" My mind had lost the power of thinking at this stage. I instantly opened the door. My whole body was numb! I saw my executioner, my lover, my life's partner, Carl! He put one foot in the door, and handed a ten-pound note to the man who had said, "Parcel delivery." It all happened so quickly: I was standing still. Carl was now inside the flat! I felt my breath had stopped, out of fear. The next thing I was aware of was waking up in my flat in Hampstead. I did not know how I got back. The last thing I remembered was Carl walking into the flat and then something hitting my face and everything going greyish black. The heavy blanket of fright was all over me. I knew I had to pay a significant price for my 'bad behaviour'. My lips were shaking, while tears were kissing my cheeks. I was sure that day that Carl was going to kill me. Then I heard the bedroom door opening and Carl was standing right there! The lava of fury was coming out from his deep blue eyes.

"I burnt all your books!" He said with pride and retribution in his voice. Then he threw some burnt papers on my face. I was sitting like a frightened mouse, at the corner of the bed. He grabbed hold of me. I closed my eyes tightly. The blows from his fists were terrible. He was pulling my hair with extreme force. He then showed me the bunch of hair that he was collecting. He kept saying, "I will break your legs, so you can't run away anymore." I had fallen on the floor by this stage. Carl started to hit my legs with his big feet. He then tried to stand up on my knees.

"Please don't," I screamed at the sight of the belt. But Carl did not stop. He, like many religious people, knew that he had a washroom: The Church, to rinse his sins away on Sunday. The blows from the belt were severely painful. Times like these in my life had made me believe in reincarnation.

I vomited with fear and pain. My screams were touching the skies, but God's hearing was temporarily out of order. My assailant did not stop, instead, he rubbed my face on the sick. Like many nights, I was prepared to die that day. I was aware that Carl would kill me, if I ever tried to escape. I was on the floor, and felt that was where I belonged! I knew if I went to the toilet to hide, it would accelerate Carl's fury. He then rushed to the toilet and got a shaver and shaved both my long eyebrows. I was mentally prepared to die that day; all I wanted was for it to be quick. *Living at the edge of life and death had torn me apart.*

Violent men like Carl, are vicious territorial animals. They absolutely regard woman as their territory, therefore no man should enter! They don't accept the meaning of an end! Therefore I knew I desperately wanted to have a peaceful end to the troubled marriage. However, I was unaware that violent relationships are not capable of producing a compromising end.

Asma Pumpi Moore

Pearl in the dust
I was locked in the prison
For the sins of my parents
Beaten to death
Day and night
I cried for help
Every bruise I got
Every punched I received
God was on his lunch break
And you were far away
Couldn't tell the world
That my world has collapsed
Once again
Then one day
The storm inside me
Broke the silence of the walls
Crushing the iron doors
I ran once more
From man-made destiny
To unknown charity
Carrying the bleeding heart
In my hand
Entered into the empty castle
The echoes of my screams
Could still follow me
I came out
Into the desert of life
To build a fortress of strength
And
To find a fountain of love
And
Discover both within myself
In the form of YOU
And
In the form of me.   *(APM)*

CRUELTY HAS NO LIMITS

There was a pin drop silence in the flat. I looked at the clock and was shocked to see that it was twenty minutes past midday. I had a burning sensation in my vagina. I felt somebody had poured vinegar and red chillies together into me. Later on I was told by the GP that I had an infection called cystitis. I called my work and explained my absence. We were living in my flat in Hampstead, and there was absolute calm outside. Apart from me, I supposed everyone had gone to work. I was getting worried that Carl did not know that I was unwell. As he suspected me all the time, he might have thought that I had run away with someone.

The vaginal pain was getting worse by the hour. I tried to stand up, but I could not. I then crawled to the toilet to wet the massive bath towel, and put that between my legs, to ease the pain. I was lying down on the bed when I heard somebody opening the door very quietly, as if they wanted to surprise the occupants. I was sure that the intruder must be a burglar. I was terrified but had no strength to fight on. I noticed that it was in fact my violently jealous husband, who thought I was with another man.

He then ran into the bedroom, but to his amazement there was no-one apart from me in the entire flat. Carl came to my side of the bed and grabbed my throat. "Who was he? Where is he hiding?" he demanded. "I knew when I called at your work that you were not in! I knew you were f***ing around."

I could not explain my situation as I was choking, literally gasping for breath. When his grip eventually loosened, I managed at last to tell him that I was not well. I explained that I had acquired a vaginal infection called cystitis; but my church-going, religious husband did not believe me. He then pulled me by the hair and told me to get up and make him a cup of coffee. I did not have the strength to do anything, and told him so. He then punched me on my left breast, and took out the bath towel from between my legs, before launching blows right at my vagina. The pain was beyond description. My screams rose in the air. I was begging him to stop, but he did not. During the struggle I fell on the floor. He grabbed hold of my legs, opened them and punched at my vagina, shouting out that I was f***ing around with someone. I kept asking him to stop, but when God does not listen to you, nobody else does! My screams were louder than the echo of my past. I cried with pain, as I had never cried before.

I married against my society and religious background. This was not my first or even my second marriage. I was devastated to accept that I had made a mistake again, this time by marrying an alcoholic. I tried to console myself that a young, lonely Asian girl in Europe was not expected to have a good sense of judgment in any case. Nobody has ever made right decisions out of loneliness. But my sense of guilt was expanding as time passed by. It was horrifying to think that I might have to end this marriage. I tried my best to communicate with Carl and asked him to go and seek professional help. But a person only seeks help if he 'believes' that he needs it.

Psychopaths like Carl do not acknowledge that they have a problem! The habit of drinking was not one that he could give up easily. For Carl it was a national heritage, it was part of his make-up.

I used to drink, occasionally, before I met Carl. It was when I saw Carl's family that I decided that nobody becomes alcoholic over night; it is a slow process that eventually overpowers a person. After seeing Carl, his father and his mother and their unreasonable behaviour because of alcohol, I decided to stop drinking. I was frightened of imagining myself like them. I decided to stop drinking at once. I did not want to lose control of my life.

Carl was a keen drinker; but was the rest caused by some of my Muslim friends who aided and abetted Carl in his bad habits? Most of them did not even tell their wives that they drank, as it is against the Islamic religion. For me it was quite fascinating to hear from their wives that their husbands had never touched alcohol. But I knew for sure that it was their husband who was completely drunk last Friday at the bar with my alcoholic husband. I was afraid to take the decision to leave Carl.

Although there was a time when I could have chosen a different path, after making a string of wrong decisions, my confidence was shattered, and my power to exercise my free will was considerably weakened. Nonetheless, as long as we are able to learn from our mistakes, we are on the road to recovery.

Birth of a son

By the mid May, I was not alone. I had an inmate. My son was born in May 1991.

Carl was very happy and promised me once again that he would not raise his hand on me. I had no option, I was hoping against hope that Carl would change his violent behaviour. However, it was not long before Carl hit me with his fist, throwing punches on my right arm. I could not do anything as I was holding the baby. I was just happy that the baby was on the left side of my chest, as I was standing. I vividly remember crying softly in the night and realising that people do not change, however, they are capable of giving wrong persona to make us look a fool.

Carl was a violent man, and would be a violent man, all I needed to do was to run away from him forever. What I could not understand was the fact that Carl was punching on my arm, and the little three month old child. In my arm was crying loudly, but it did not stop the father to stop hitting his wife. Since that I strongly believe that any man who can't care for his own child, would not care for any one in the world.

Carl's violent attitude did not stop at me, soon he started to shake the baby if he cried aloud. Although I was not a child psychologist, however, it was clear to me that the treatment my son was receiving in the hands of his father was not good.

Carl's favourite punishment was to lock me in the toilet, if I ever run to escape from his violent attacks. Now it was more disturbing as one day I was in the kitchen and Mykey (son) was in the bed room with Carl. However the crying noise was coming from the toilet door. I ran to the toilet and found out that the baby was lying on the floor. When I asked Carl what happened how did the baby ended up in the toilet. He replied to me that the baby was winging therefore he put the baby in the toilet and switch off the light so he can learn his lesson. I was furious at Carl's way of punishment.

My only connection to the outside world was the phone and Liz, the woman who lived downstairs. However, after calling the police from the house a few times, Carl told me that he was going to punish me for dialling 999. I was shocked one day when, after finishing breakfast, he unplugged the phone and put it in a Sainsbury's carrier bag. I asked him what he was doing. At first he smiled then went to the kitchen. He took out a fork and plucked out my hair from the roots. His actions were so quick and frightfully painful, I was screaming. He then smiled at me and said " Now call your f***ing English police!" After this it was normal for Carl to take the phone to work, so I had nothing to communicate with. My screams had made my son wake up. As I looked at him I was glad that at least I had the most precious thing of my life with me!

Once I was having a bath while Mykey was fast asleep and Carl was in the bedroom. Then I heard the child crying. Mother's intuition told me that there was something wrong. I ran out of the bathroom and saw that the child's hands were tied with Carl's tie. Carl's explanation was that the child kept throwing clothes from the drawer, while Carl was closing the drawer, and Mykey had kept opening the drawer.

I said to him, "That's what children do." I then tried to loosen the tie from his tiny hands. Carl came running towards me and grabbed hold of my head. He then punched me on my cheek, and pushed me away from the child. As I fell down I was kicked badly, on my back, over and over again. He kept saying that it was important to control the child this way, otherwise he would turn into a spoilt brat later on.

By this time the child was crying intensely. His cries sounded extremely painful, and he was hyperventilating. I felt exceptionally helpless. If I could not defend an eighteen-month-old baby, what prospects did I have of rescuing myself?

As a child seeing my parents unhappy in their marriage was painful for me. Somehow we, the children, blamed ourselves for their reason to be together. Their verbal abuse affected our studies. It was amazing to see that human beings can breathe air, with so much pollution by anxiety and hatred around them.

As children, three brothers and four sisters, all seven of us used to sit together in one room. As soon as their argument started, no matter what each one of us was doing, we used to stop and sit in one bedroom. It was like an unspoken law of solidarity. We sisters used to cry, but I remember my brothers used only to bite their nails. I was determined that I would never be married and have children. For a child to see his/her parents showing verbal hatred for each other is devastating. A child could run to one of the parents, should he/she have had a fight with a sibling: but where do you go when parents fight?

I was desperate to leave Carl. I felt like a fish with out water. I was asking for help, but no one was listening, or may be the fear suppressed my voice.

CHAPTER SIX

THE POLICE

CARL THREATENED ME that if I ever called the police, he would kill me. I thought that, even without provocation Carl was brutally violent towards me, so what would he do if I annoyed him? The consequence of that was too horrific to imagine. Carl and his parents told me that if the police became involved in a domestic incident, they would take our child, and he would be put in to care, until the matter was resolved. The consequences were too high to risk. I could not take that risk. Ignorance can make you pay a lot in terms of emotions. As I was not born in this country, I did not know the laws. I had only been in England for two years, when I met my husband.

Carl told me that the police could not put him in jail for life. Eventually, one day, when he got out, he would pour acid over me. He told me that he knew ruthless people in Ealing, who were the members of the IRA, and it was very easy for him to finish me off and get rid of my body. Therefore I had no choice. My biggest fear at that stage was the safety of my son. I knew I had to live for my son.

It was 1991, Mykey was few months old. I took him to the pond in Hampstead. As we were feeding the ducks, I could not fail to notice, how quickly and accurately, ducklings were dipping their heads in the water, imitating the mother duck. For me it was another waking up call that Mykey would become another Carl Moore, should I stay in this

What if?

violent relationship, as Carl's behaviour was the exact copy of a home life where men beat their women, and use the Bible as their shield. I was boiling with anger at the fact that religion seemed to be some men's tool of oppression. The name of the tool may differ from culture to culture. Although, from other people's point of view, it may seem an easy option to walk out on a violent partner, however, the ultimate fear that your violent partner would find you and kill you was as certain as death itself – and it's the fear that prevents the escape. I kept thinking at least I could be around my son, so what if I had a bruised breast, and arm.

As time was passing by Carl's violence was getting worse. I had no family support. And as far as Carl's family was concerned, they were extremely proud of his behaviour, because, according to them the Bible gave him the authority to raise his hand to me. I was a bad wife, who did not 'obey' her master. It was hard for me to accept the irrational aspects of a religion in a country where even dogs have rights.

It was 8pm, on a normal working day. I was busy washing up, as our flat had an open plan kitchen and living room. I could see Mykey was playing on the floor. Carl was watching television at the time, in the same room. Mykey started to cry for something. I asked Carl to pick up the child. And the next thing I saw Carl threw a bunch of keys at him to shut him up. As Carl used to work as a handy man in different people's houses, he had many keys in that bunch. The key ring hit Mykey right on his little face, and immediately blood began to flow. We rushed him to the hospital, Carl told me on the way to the hospital, if I told the doctor or nurse what had really happened, the child would go to the care home. I was supposed to say he fell on the ground and hit his forehead. I had no choice but to agree with Carl. When the doctor saw Mykey, Carl was so convincing, that even for a moment I thought Mykey had fallen.

I was fully aware of the fact that Mykey was in real danger, day and night, emotionally, as well as physically, as a direct result of this marriage. I needed to escape, if not for my sake, then for the sake of the child who was unable to defend himself. Most violent men are cowards, as they do not accept their mistakes. They refuse to admit that they may be in the wrong, and Carl was no exception to that.

It was a cold winter evening in December. I was sitting on the sofa and had a chair in front of me, on which I was resting my outstretched legs. Suddenly I noticed a big bruise on my leg. Carl walked into the room, and as he was in a perfectly good mood, I showed him the bruise on my leg, given by him.

That changed everything. He left the room and suddenly came back with a massive bag and dropped it on my knee. "You want to talk about bruises and spoil the evening? Alright, I'll give you some bruises," he said confidently. The severe pain numbed my tongue, and froze my mind. I could not move for hours. "Don't show me your bloody bruises as they have got nothing, absolutely nothing, to do with me, you made me do that," he shouted, trying to justify himself.

It came to the stage where I thought that even if I complained to God, the psychopath would hear it and punish me for opening my mouth. You keep your mouth sealed and die bit by bit every day. It is a reluctant form of euthanasia.

We were living in Maiden Lane, Camden, while Carl's parents were still lived in Ireland, however, they were the very frequent visitors to our home. Which Carl and I enjoyed. I never had argument with them, in fact we used to enjoy each other's company and share racist jokes and laugh together. I only had problem when they bring religion into our marriage and justify Carl's violent behaviour.

It was one of those visits of Carl's parent to London, in 1991, when Carl informed me with great pride that he and his father had decided that I should go and work. I was not only angry, but furious, as I felt I was in Pakistan. Where men decide women's destiny! Carl was very proud to inform me that his father told him to stop buying food for the house, then she had to go and earn money to survive. I did not think they could be serious. But unfortunately they were. Carl stopped shopping for food altogether. I was not working and I had no knowledge that I could even claim any benefit. I was from a country where it's hard to earn money, for people like me, it was inconceivable that one would get paid if he or she is not working.

There were many days when I had nothing in the house to eat. My son was on breast feeding, which made me more weaker. Carl used to eat at different pubs before coming home. I had no way to generate money while looking after my beautiful baby. However, I was amazed to find this contradiction in my personality that on one hand, I wanted to show off my legs like Western girls, on the other hand, I was like a traditional Asian mother, whose sole purpose of living is her children.

Life was getting worse each day. I knew I had to go out and work, but for me, my child's upbringing was my prime concern. The weeks went by and I had few potatoes in the basket. Mykey was on breast milk, therefore, I used to get as hungry as a pig. I could not believe at my luck, out of the frying pan into the fire. My Filipino friend, Vikki, lived a few doors away. She often used to call me to have lunch with her; she was my only hope for food. But then there were days when she was busy, and I had nothing except boiled or fried potatoes.

I then went to Vikki's house and gave her a list to buy some food, as I could not go shopping with the baby. I knew she would not ask me for the money upfront, and in the evening when she brought the shopping, Carl had to give her the money. The plan worked, but coming back from Vikki's flat I felt angry with myself. I let myself down.

I was a strong girl before I met Carl Moore. I had fantastic managerial positions. There was a time when I was in charge of 25 male staff, in one of London's Indian restaurants During 1988 I was the General Manageress of 12 hotels in Victoria, London. I failed to understand how on one hand I could be so strong outside my home, while inside I was like a timid mouse. I had the same fear of going to my matrimonial home, as I had when I was a little girl, with the fear of my mother. I vividly remember wondering whether it was love that took my energy, or was I losing my mind, or could it be what Mother infested in my brain all through my life that, beating is what I really deserve?

CHAPTER SEVEN

Cul-de-sac

It was early one Saturday evening when I finished cleaning the kitchen floor with the cloth. I took the cloth to the toilet to wash it as I never wash dirty clothes in the kitchen sink. I entered the toilet and saw Carl was soaking in bubbles. I was washing the cloth, when Carl asked me to wash it in the kitchen sink. I simply refused as it is unhygienic. The next thing I heard was a big splash! Carl leapt out of the bath and pulled my hair, exactly like my mother used to do. He then slapped me across my face. I ran out of the bathroom to the living room. But this cruel man did not leave me alone. He came after me, and this time he kicked me on my leg and I was on the floor. He grabbed my hair and hit my head against the wall. I screamed with excruciating pain. I tried to fight him. I tried to kick his legs. But it was not easy; I was on the floor and my assailant was a six-foot-tall Irish builder. I escaped again. I ran to the telephone, which was at the end of the corridor. As soon as I grabbed it, Carl's foot crushed my tiny hands. He kept kicking me. I took my hand from the receiver and cried bitterly. Carl punched my face.

I was on the floor, my only thought was to get hold of a gun! I am sure if I'd had a gun at any time during my violent relationship with Carl, he would not be alive today. I could hear my helpless boy's crying in the background. Nevertheless, it was his crying that was making me go on and fight the battle. I got up, much faster this time, and ran out of the flat. I couldn't go to Liz, the Scots woman who often saved my son and me, as she didn't have a phone.

I ran to the street. I then found a public phone. My jaw was hurting severely. I dialled 999! The aching jaw prevented me from speaking. I kept crying, holding the phone in my hand. Meanwhile the police managed to trace my call. Within few minutes I heard a police siren and saw flashing lights. It was as if God had come to rescue me. I felt safe! The police tried their best to find out what had happened to me and who had done it, but I could not speak, my jaw was aching more than my heart. Then one of the officers handed me his notebook and pen. I wrote, with my hand shaking, what had happened. They took me to hospital. While I was in the police van, I remember one of the officer asking me, "Was he drunk?" I was puzzled at his question, how could he have known that Carl was drunk? I wrote this in the notebook. "We see this kind of thing every week end, in different houses," replied one of the officers. I was horrified to know that there were many 'moore'!

"It gets worse with time," the officer affirmed. I was terrified of my return and devastated to leave my son behind. The police asked me several times to write my address but I was petrified that Carl would kill me if he knew that I had called the police. "Please just take me to the hospital." I wrote my request in the notebook.

The police took me to the Whittington Hospital, London, where I received treatment. While I was in one of the cubicles, one of the officers came to me and told me that his father used to hit his mother, and his mother had left him nine years ago, and she had been happy ever since. He assured me that it was worth it. "Mrs Moore, if you are thinking that he will change, you are kidding yourself! Change is in your hands! You can change your life by leaving him. Don't forget we are stronger than we think!" the police officer said. He left a powerful message with me. Police traced our home address from the hospital and informed me that the child was safe. I was treated for my jaw in the hospital. After words a nurse came to my room to inform me that my husband was at the reception to pick me up. I was petrified. My lips started to shake, however, I was desperate to see my child. The nurse told me that he was very upset and apologetic. I was worried, I asked the nurse to bring the baby and then I could go hide some where. I just wanted to run away, but there was nowhere I could go. The nurse came back and told me that "Your husband was not leaving the baby, he asked you to come home with him: he seems very upset." Nurse was feeling sorry for him. I knew it was all acting. I wanted to get away from Carl. I knew I would face a very angry man at home. I wanted to run away, but there was no place to hide. It is hard to believe but it is true to say that when trying to trace an old friend, the world seems like such a huge planet, however, when running from a psychopath the world seems more like a fish bowl.

I had no other choice but to follow the nurse to meet my assailant, and go home with him to be beaten again. I was still not able to speak a word due to my injured jaw, however inside me the screams were unbearable. Once we arrived at home, Maiden Lane, Carl was not that apologetic and sad man. He was the man who follow his old tradition to control 'his wife'. On our arrival Carl plucked some of my hair with the fork, as if he was picking spaghetti. He plucked my hair from the roots, it was the most excrutiating pain. All I could hear was the child screaming in the back ground and running toward me. Carl kicked the child with full force. My mind was exploding with anger. However I could not do anything, as Carl was holding me tight. My son's screaming were making me strong I knew the time was not far when I would be free.

Carl looked at the hair he plucked then laughed and said, "Now call your bastard British Police". He kept plucking my hair. By 2am both Carl and Mykey fell asleep. Although the flat was silent but in my ears it was my son's screaming. I was determined to leave him: did not know how and when, but I knew I WILL one day!

I was living in constant fear, however, Mykey was the only light in the dark days of my life.

It was August 1992, the gusts of an 100-mile-an-hour wind across London and the South East, had uprooted giant trees and brought human traffic to a standstill. Hundreds of car accidents were reported on television. Police were warning motorists not to travel unless it was an emergency. Carl had gone to work and he was supposed to have been back three hours ago. I was worried about his safety. I tried to convince myself that I would be better off if he didn't come home! By now it was midnight. There was no phone call or message on the answer phone. I was praying for his safe return when at about 12:45am, I saw a car coming towards the Maiden Lane flats, I felt a great relief that he was fine and alive. "Hi. How are you? Carl, why didn't give me a call? I was worried sick!" I asked with concern.

Carl was walking towards the living room, then suddenly he turned and *Tashhh*! A big fist greeted me on my face. I was glued to the door. I was hurt as I had been praying for his safety all evening! He then grabbed my cheeks and held them far apart.

"Don't f***ing talk to me like you are my mother. You are not my mother. I am not your child that has to inform you about my whereabouts," shouted Carl.

He kept holding my cheeks apart and then he punched my stomach. He then started to throw things about and I was scared that it would wake the baby up.

"Don't make a noise, the child is sleeping," I said.

My sentence made him aware that there was another vulnerable person who could be the target! He ran to the bedroom where the child was sleeping. I was about to get up when I heard a *bang*! I ran to the bedroom, as I was running, I heard the child screaming. I entered the room and saw the double bed was on my four months old baby. It was a miracle that the child was safe. I grabbed him and ran to another room and dialled 999. The child was terrified and crying endlessly. His cries were too distressing to bear, as he was gasping for breath. I was petrified that the police might put the child into care, as Carl and his parents had told me. But I knew at the same time the only safety net was the presence of the police! The sound of the police radio was coming from the stairs, as we were living on the second floor. I was holding the child close to my chest. Carl kept trying to take the child out of my arms.

He did not look like the man I fell in love with. The smell of beer was too strong and the fire from his eyes was telling me that he had some other plans. I was scared for the safety of myself and the child, but then the loud knock at the door... *tap tap* ... "Open up It is the POLICE !" As soon as Carl heard the radio, he ran like a mouse and jumped off the balcony. I opened the door and saw three police officers standing there.

The child was still crying endlessly. One of the police officers took the child from my arms and I was terrified because I thought, "That's it! Now they were going to take the child away." "Please don't take my child!" I pleaded to the officer.

"Don't worry he is safe, he is not going anywhere, why don't you go and get water for yourself and the baby?" The officer smiled and said he was not going to take the child away. Later that evening one of the officers came close to me, "Can I ask you why you are with him?" he asked.

"Because I love him and he loves me," I replied.

"Is this what you call love? Beating you every week?" The officer questioned my loyalty.

"It is not an English marriage where you leave each other just because you are bored," I answered with sarcasm.

"Mrs Moore, ask yourself, are you in the marriage to start with? Marriage means two people living together loving and respecting each other!" The officer challenged me with his solid question.

The two officers who ran to chase Carl brought him back to the flat within minutes. The police then asked me if I wanted to press charges? I was about to say yes, when I saw

Carl, standing behind the police officer and showing his FIST! My answer quickly changed from yes to no!

The police officers left the flat, but the words of that police officer made a building block in my decision to get out of that so-called marriage. I was beginning to believe that my son and I deserved a better life. Therefore I was determined at that time to do something and have a life not an existence!

It was late 1992. By this time I realized that I had to make the best out of the mess of my life. I knew I could not afford to take any more chances on my life to run away from my assailant, as I had responsibility for a child. I decided to seek help from Carl's parents. We arrived at their house in Woodlands, in December 1992.

The house was glittering with Christmas lights. I was determined to seek the help of Carl's parents with regard to Carl's violent behaviour. But before I could even ask, I was the target of Carl's violence once more, this time in front of them. Carl brutally slapped me across my face, when I simply refused to go the pub with his family due to sheer tiredness. I was amazed to see that both parents could sit, and watch his abusive behaviour. Their attitude was as peaceful, as an old couple watching swans on the river.

I took the child and ran to the bedroom, where Carl and his parents followed me. Carl's parents were condemning Carl for not being able to control me. I was holding Mykey on my arm, who was only one and a half years old. When Carl started to punch at my arm. Mykey started to cry bitterly, Carl always detested a child's cry, he quickly grabbed the child and threw him at the bed. I covered him with myself as soon as I saw Carl pulling out his belt from his trousers, so the child would not get the strikes from the belt. The blows from the belt slashed my back, while I was knocking at God's closed door. I believed Carl was hitting me to prove to his parents that he could control his wife.

"Jesus Christ, what do you expect your husband to do when you don't listen to him, even the Bible says that a man should control his wife?" Carl's mother shouted.

My cries were without any tears, like a severe wound, with internal bleeding. I was beginning to believe that the lava of my anger would burst at any time, but did not know, at what price?

The blows from the belt did not let me sleep. The pain of my back was like somebody peeling my skin with sharp nails and pouring vinegar at the same time. I did not know the crime, for which I was being punished. The next day, I managed to pluck up the courage to ask his parents about their pride in their son's obnoxious behaviour.

"You are lucky your husband only uses his fist and belt, when I was young and upset Carl's father, he would beat me up with the fire poker, sometimes with a belt. See a man has got to control his woman!" Carl's mother calmly replied. Her conviction confirmed what I read long time ago, "Men are what their mothers make them".

I was horrified to bring up my son in an atmosphere where there was no respect for women. "In the Bible it says that women should be chastised… if she disobeys her husband!" Carl's father very proudly added, with a bitter smile on his face. His words slashed my heart, especially, as they were coming from a Western man!

Last Christmas

I knew about Carl's background, therefore it was vital to comprehend that Carl's chances of his recovery from his violent behaviour were quite slim. I suggested to him, that once we were back in England, we should seek a divorce. In a Catholic household, the word divorce is a swear word, which is prohibited. Carl's parents went absolutely crazy. Carl's mother came towards me and grabbed the child from me. His father asked Carl to drop me at the train station, and let me figure out how to go back to London. I knew that I would not leave their house without my son in my arms. Carl's mother took the child to the kitchen. I sat there and wept. Carl and his father followed her into the kitchen. As Christmas was only few days away. We were supposed to go to Newport, to celebrate Christmas with all the relatives but the tension in the Moores' residence was increasing, all the time. Nobody talked to me all morning. I knew they were up to some plan. I was petrified for my son and my safety. I only knew one thing, that I did not know anything about Ireland. I did not even know the emergency number. The silence in the house was like a silence before the storm!

I could smell fear. The next morning I woke up and noticed neither his parents nor Carl were in the living room. The house was like a haunted place. I could sense, that they would not let me take the child, their 'grandson' with me. I was beginning to question my wellbeing. I tiptoed towards the kitchen door. I could feel my heart was pounding. I could hear people talking in the kitchen. "I am telling you, you will never see the child any other way. Her sister lives in New York, what happens if she takes the child there?" Carl's mother suggested to Carl. "Son, you can't afford to lose a son, it's one of us, a Moore." Carl's father said with his utmost pride.

Carl interrupted, "Mother, I hit her but I don't hate her. I love her very much I really can't kill her. Be real do you really think no one is going to know?" Carl said with a dead sad voice. I felt somebody was cutting at my heart with a blunt knife. My whole body was numb. If they killed me then nobody would know that I had disappeared. Although I had had enough of life by this time, the thought of Mykey being raised in an alcoholic family, with people who had no morals, was devastating me.

"Son, she is going to take your son. You will never be able to see your child," Carl's mother warned him.

"Listen Carl, the simple way is the rat poison," His father asserted.

"Exactly, that's what your father and I were discussing last night," his mother told Carl.

I then heard Carl's voice, "What am I going to tell her family? What about the dead body?"

"She does not believe in any religion, why can't you just say that she asked to be cremated!" His father said. By this time both parents were laughing loudly.

"Carl, I can take care of that side. If you want, you and your father can go to Dublin, for a few days, you are self-employed, she does not work, what's the hurry? I can handle it." Carl's mother reassured him. I went to the bedroom. My whole body was shivering with fever! I was in a foreign land, where I did not know anybody. The only people I knew were planning to finish my life. I had no money. I was alone at their mercy. That was the moment when I felt how people in concentration camps must have felt. The only desire to be alive!

The house was at a remote location. None of my friends even knew the address. I realized that the walk from their house to the high street would be impossible. Even if I got there what was I going to do?

I decided that I had to be calm and try to find some help from somewhere. Suddenly like lightning a thought came: to call someone for whom you need no number. I called God, through faith. I put my child's safety and myself in His hands.

I then felt a little courage, and decided to play obedient until I got to England. I decided not to let them know that I had heard what they were planning. Although I could not stop biting my nails and moistening my lips. While my legs were shaking, with terror and fear, I could not sit for more than two minutes. The fright of poisoning by Carl's mother compelled me to starve myself for two whole days; the only food I could trust was the biscuits in the jar in our bedroom.

It was December 22nd 1992. Christmas was three days away. I was very weak due to lack of food and the fear. The whole family was acting kindly towards me at this time, which was more frightening for me. They kept insisting that I should eat something, I pretended that I had a bad stomach. I could not sleep during the night, as I did not know the outcome of their wicked plan. Mobile phones in 1992 were not as accessible as today. I have a good memory for telephone numbers, but there was no chance to call anyone for help, as I did not know the dialling code from Ireland to England. However, it was a great relief to sense that communicating with God does not require any man-made gadgets. There are times in our lives when we pray from our heart, and there are times when every pore of our body prays and our spirit joins us as well and that powerful prayer does reach to God! I never liked the greasy taste of chocolates, but hunger has its own palate. And after twelve hours of hunger, chocolates tasted marvellous. The rigid atmosphere was still unnerving. The silence of terror was extremely intense, it was sending shivers in my spine.

I then decided to turn the tables. I decided that I had to be nice to them, to make them believe that I would never leave their son, Carl. To make them believe in me, I had to apologize to each one of them. I knew I had to sail across the other side and this was the only boat available. I had only two options. I knew I was not compromising my convictions, I was taking the right route for the safety of my child!

Sorry seems to be the hardest word!

Asking forgiveness is hard, but when you are not in the wrong, it is the hardest. I realized, that I had to be in England to leave Carl. I also knew that I had to get out of Ireland in one piece to fight my battle for freedom. I realized by then that Irish society was as bad as Asian society, the judiciary was played by men, not by the laws.

I went down to the living room. The television was switched off, the lights on the Christmas tree were burning like the anger inside my heart. Christmas was only forty-eight hours away. All the Christmas presents were lying under the tree. It was sad to see so much darkness around me, despite all those lights. I took a deep breath, pushed my ego aside. I sat next to Carl. "I am really sorry, you are right, I am mad. I am sorry to have upset all of you. I can't afford to go through another divorce. Please Carl, don't ever leave me, I promise I will do exactly what you ask me to." Carl kept quiet, and I continued to apologize, "Please give me one last chance!" I said. But in my heart I said, "B******, let me go to England, the country where women can live! I would kick you out of my life."

I felt bad as Carl started to cry and said, "I really love you but I can't stop myself when I am mad." "You provoked him, that is the reason he lashed out at you," his father interrupted. I ignored all that. I was like a fine chess player, counting and calculating every move. Instead of replying, I apologized to Carl's parents. I knew in my heart that was the last time I would be in their house. I could see that Carl's parents were not very sure about my convictions. But for me it was a relief to know that I convinced Carl I would not leave him. Instead I was begging him to stay in my life. I knew if you want to make an Irishman happy, you take him to the pub. I asked to go to the pub.

In the pub, I asked Carl's parents to visit England in May for Mykey's second birthday. The next moment I told them that, after Mykey's second birthday, we would think about having another child. I think that was the ultimate gesture from me, for a long-term commitment, from Carl's parents' point of view. I could see that they were very relaxed and convinced.

What if?

I then asked them, "Why don't we eat here, rather than going home?" They all agreed and for the first time in three days, I ate a full meal. The feeling was fabulous. Carl agreed to go back to London with Mykey and me in three days time. The wait for those three days, was the longest period of my entire life! The day we arrived in London I felt like a prisoner on death row feels when he receives clemency. I was determined not to waste this chance.

A bruised jaw recorded on a party photograph.

CHAPTER EIGHT

Sanity v insanity

Although Carl did not agree with his parents to kill me, my trust in him was totally gone. The first few weeks after the return from Ireland were fine, but then Carl was back to his normal routine of abuse. Carl was determined to destroy me mentally. I was still hanging in there but waiting for the right time to escape from that prison. Carl's attitude was getting worse. Exactly as the Metropolitan Police officers had warned me. Carl started to tell me that I was losing my mind. I therefore should go to the doctor and get some medicine for my mental illness! The statement was very strong, but without any substantial evidence. I told him that it was not true. Carl insisted that he would prove to me that I was losing my mind. Although I was petrified of Carl's way of thinking, I carried on as normally as possible. I did not have a driving licence, but I had many driving lessons before I met Carl. It was my driving test next day. I went to put petrol in the car, with Carl, as I did not have the full licence at that time. Next day my friend Kim came to take me to the test centre, but when we tried to start the car, it would not start! "The petrol needle is showing there is no petrol in the car," Kim explained, after looking at the dial.

I was astounded! I was quite sure that I did put the petrol in last night! Carl came near the car to ask us what was happening. I, obviously, asked him if he could remember my putting the petrol in the car last night. "I came back at 11pm last night, how could you go with me for petrol, darling? In fact, you were fast asleep when I got back." Kim was very shocked to hear Carl's version, but the authority in his voice convinced both of us that I was wrong.

It was about 1:30pm on early Saturday afternoon when Carl received a phone call from Heathrow Airport that his parents were waiting for us to go and pick them up. It was a surprise, because normally they inform us well in advance. About 7pm Carl came back from Heathrow Airport, along with his parents. Carl's parents were claiming that they did speak to me the night before and told me about their programme and that they would be arriving at 1pm the next day. I was confused and shocked at the same time. I did not remember speaking to them at all! Carl was determined that I did speak to them. At that stage I started to disbelieve myself; in fact, I started to feel frightened for myself. It was one of the chilliest nights in London. I was busy preparing the dinner. Suddenly, I heard a child's scream. I ran to the toilet where the screams were coming from and saw Carl and the baby. Carl was trying to pull the baby out of the bath! The water was extremely cold! The baby was not wearing any clothes. I was terrified to see my son in that condition. "You must go and see a psychiatrist, you desperately need some help," Carl shouted with confidence. At first it did not make any sense. Carl then said that I left the baby in the cold bath! "I did not touch the child," I clearly stated. Carl kept insisting that he was on the balcony, and the child was too young to climb into the bath, so it had to be me. The assurance in his voice was enough for me to doubt myself. It was the first time in my entire life that I doubted myself! I then burst into tears! He then said to me that I didn't need to worry about anything, he was not going to tell the social services, as long as I went to seek psychiatric help and get some medicine.

My confidence was being sucked up by the revelation from Carl that I was a mental case. My strong heart and my questioning mind was all I ever had! He told me that we should go to live in Ireland, because in English Law they might take the child if I ended up in a mental hospital. I was like a puppet who was in the hands of this wild manipulative creature. I never doubt two things in my life: one of them is the existence of God, and the other my faith in myself. But at that time I was losing both!

The next day, when Carl went to work I went to see my old friend Tony and told him about my so-called psychological problems. Tony was a wise person; he was the one who opened my eyes and showed me that it was only Carl and his family who were doing all that to me. Tony explained how easy it was for them to collaborate in their story, to make me believe that I was insane. He explained to me how easy it could be for Carl to take out the petrol from the car in the night! How easy it was for his parents to corroborate his story by saying that they had called from Ireland and you spoke to them!

I could not believe that anybody could make such ruthless accusations about another person. I called one of Carl's uncles and his wife in Ireland, Sammy and Mary, who had always been impartial. Sammy and Mary confirmed my fears. Carl's parents had told them that Pumpi was being recommended to a psychiatric hospital and very soon Michael (junior) would be looked after by Carl and his parents in Ireland. They believed it would be good for Michael, as in England he was not getting any Catholic teaching. I was disappointed in their devious thinking and planning. I was still in disbelief; the mere fact that a father could deprive the child of his mother, and a father could play a part in destroying his son's home was beyond my imagination. Life never stops surprising us! I was afraid for my safety, but above all, I was petrified for my little boy's future. I knew the time had come for me to make a decision, before a decision was made for me. I looked up at the sky and thought: one could change the country, but not the luck! I was afraid to have a cup of tea Carl had made for me. I was getting frightened as I could see Carl's desperation to get rid of me in a devious manner. I had to make sure I had a neighbour, colleague or friend with me as much as possible. Carl's attitude in front of other people was very charming. He was a good actor. Life was becoming very frustrating, as home is usually the only place where one can feel happy and relaxed, but in my case it was the place that hurt me the most. I was like most domestic violence victims, wishing for a miracle, a magic spell that could put everything right and be as beautiful as it was when we first met!

THE JOB CENTRE

I knew I had to earn some money. I did not have money to buy food, clothes or even to get my hair cut. I looked like a tramp. However, on the surface, we were like any happily married couple. I decided to go back to work, as the child was two years old. I could not go for the interview as I never had money for a bus pass or for someone to look after the child for that matter. Then one day I was explaining to Liz how much I wanted to go back to work, Liz was a very sweet and kind woman; she straight away offered to look after the boy. I told her that I would pay her when I got my first pay cheque. Liz looked after Mykey whenever I went out for the job interviews plus lent me money from her little 'giro cheque'. I was desperate to find a job and luckily in April 1993, I found one in a Job Centre, Camden Town, as an admin officer. Coming back to the labour market was another hurdle, as I lacked self confidence by now. I was very aware of my bruises; even if it was hot weather I had to make sure I wore a long skirt to hide my bruises. Nevertheless, I knew I would regain strength one day.

The final straw

I was reading the paper, when I saw Mykey running nude and Carl running after him. I put the newspaper down and gazed at the game. To my amazement the game was called 'Catch the nono' (the penis). Both father and son were nude. Although the weather was hot, there was still no justification for such a filthy game. Here I was, teaching a two-year-old child that this was his private part so don't let anybody touch it – while on the other hand, his father was teaching him that it was something a child should let his father play with. What a contrast in parental behaviour under the same roof! Carl told me that I was a very old-fashioned Asian woman. But for some reason I felt disgusted by that game. And I was more surprised, when he told me that he had played this before and the child loved it. I put my foot down and distracted Mykey. After that day, I was on full alert.

Money is everything. Being everything, it is nothing!
—APM

On my payday Carl asked me to make sure that the pay would go to the joint account. I knew money would make me strong, and secure. I needed to get rid of him. Money not only gives you comfort: but it enables you to open your senses too!

He was very aggressive before my payday. And I knew that if the money went to my account I would be beaten to death; but I also knew that if it went to our joint account, it would go on gambling machines and drinking. I was worried and confused. I then decided to give him his own medicine – lie. I came back the next day and told Carl with some artificial anger that, " I can't believe it is my money, but they can't put it where I want! Can you believe the b****** said that the joint account has two names and on the cheque there is only one name, therefore it has to go to my personal account."

Carl did not believe me at first, but then I gave her my colleague's name to confirm it. I knew he would never have the guts to confront anybody outside the house. People like Carl are a lion at home but in front of other people they are perfect gentlemen. My clever thinking worked. I started to save money, and began making plans to leave him forever.

In the past whenever I tried to lock the doors from inside, he always managed to climb through the window or unlock the door from outside. And I was beaten badly afterwards. Therefore I was very calculating this time. It was a very pleasant Friday evening and my son was sleeping. I was sitting on the balcony. Carl was in the pub as usual. I had my friend Liz with me and I was sharing my plans with her. Liz was a great Scottish person. I knew she was my secret keeper. Then we saw two policemen talking to an old woman. I told Liz that he was the one who gave me the lecture about leaving Carl. I ran downstairs and told him that I had a job. He was delighted. I then told him that I would leave Carl one day, but in the past when I locked the door he could still open the door. Both the officers were very kind. They came upstairs to check the lock in our flat, as Carl was away. They told me that the lock was not strong enough. Even a child could break it. One of them advised me to swap it with one of your good friend's on the night you want to close the chapter on him. "When he tries to get in," they told me, "you call 999, and we will arrest him. As he will not have the keys of the flat, that should give you enough time to escape or stay safe!" Both officers left, leaving me to decide about my future.

However, I kept thinking about the paradox of the game of life! The person who thought that life is nothing without you, was about to take your life?

Sick game or sick mind?

It was about 6pm. Carl was having a bath for a very long time. Carl often took Mykey for a bath, with him and it was one of those days. I opened the bathroom door to see if they had gone sleep! As I opened the door I saw Carl was lying in the bath with his penis erect at 90 degrees and, to my surprise, being held by the two-year-old child. I was shocked and speechless.

What if?

Carl looked at my amazement: "What?"

"You bastard!" I shouted. I was as still as a dead body. Then I burst into tears and screamed.

"Look! What is the big deal? You let him suck your tits! It is only a game! Watch! Watch! Mykey tickle my balls," Carl proclaimed with laughter.

I was disgusted to see that he had trained a child to give him sexual pleasure. Mykey was happily touching his balls and both father and son were laughing at this game. I felt sick. I grabbed the child, like an eagle snatching a young offspring from the nest! I could not sleep all night. I was sobbing all night. I knew Carl would not be in the house tomorrow night. I made that long overdue decision. My fear was still there, but the burning desire to fight until I die for the safety of my child overrode every fear I ever had.

In the night I was shaking with anger. I had never experienced that much anger ever in myself. It was incomprehensible that a human being could still function carrying such a burden of anger. I wanted to kill him immediately. My whole body was sweating and I needed a knife or a gun to shoot him. I went to the kitchen and tried to hold the knife. It was ironic that I heard my son's cry at that moment. I then realized, "Who was going to look after this innocent life? He did not ask to be born. What was his crime?" I knew in the morning I had to make the decision of a lifetime!

My anger had reached its peak. By now, I was a different person. I set aside my sentiments as does a soldier when he goes to war. I declared war against my enemy! My country was my child! But the enemy was within!

An eye for an eye

It was 1993, a very hot day in June. I left my son with my friend, as I knew it was judgment day for Carl. It was just after 7pm, I was desperately waiting for Carl to come home. I was fuming with anger. I wanted to make Carl drunk and then physically torture him, before leaving him forever. The rage and anger had blinded me at the time. Carl arrived home about eight. I took out all the beer from the fridge, and offered him a drink. I knew that Carl became very angry when he drinks too much, but I also knew that if he crossed the next line, he becomes very passive! I wanted him to get to the second stage. I did not need to wait too long. After hours of drinking, Carl was practically unconscious. I knew if he was at his normal strength, I would not be able to fight him. I ran to the bedroom and tore a bed sheet. He did not resist while I tied his hands. Carl was lying on the floor like a dead body. Then I put my four-inch heels on Carl's back, pressing them hard.

"This is how it felt when you stabbed me with the fork, just because the potatoes were not cooked properly!" I explained.

"This is how you walked over me for five long suffering years, bastard." I said with fury in each word. I then got hold of his boots and slashed them across his face.

"This is how I felt when you kicked me with these boots!" I screamed at him. I was not Pumpi that night. Here was a power of ultimate rage, coming out with the speed of light! My fear of Carl had turned into fury – giving me endless power.

I had flashbacks of five years of physical, mental, and

sexual abuse! While my only crime was to love him endlessly! I was shouting out of my stomach. I then opened his legs, and then kicked his balls. "This is the reminder of my vaginal infection, when you kicked me, bastard, right where I was suffering," I reminded him.

Carl was in severe pain. He was pulling his feet towards his stomach. I then kicked him again and again in his back. My tears and screaming were at their peak. I was sure that I was going to kill him. It was a long held retribution. I knew this was my first and last chance. I was getting out of breath by this time. I looked at the state of Carl, and felt as if my wounds were smiling, while my tears were laughing at my courage. I then got his weapon, the leather belt. I was neither happy nor sad to see him turning and twisting, but I had a sense of satisfaction.

My torture on Carl had started at eight, and with several intervals, it was now six o'clock in the morning. I had left Mykey with my friend for the night as I knew the night could twist any way. I had no strength left in my body. My hands were aching, and legs were shaking. I knew he was still alive. Blood was coming from Carl's nose and face, but I did not feel anything. My senses were over powered by anger. I then dragged his half-dead body, out of the flat, and with all my hatred I pushed him out of the door! The door, where he promised on our son's head that he would never raise his hand to me. I then took out his tools, and changed the locks as suggested by the police officer! That was the end of my third marriage!

It was baffling, even for myself, to perceive that at the age of twenty-six, I had been married three times, and at the age of twenty-nine, had left three husbands! I was numb for a whole week. I did not even have the strength to feed the child. But in my heart I knew I could not afford to let the heartaches of my life be the obstacles to my dreams. I needed to change anger and hurt into a vehicle of force that would take me to the road to recovery! I was determined to give my child a home where he could be free to run around, not live in fear of being locked in the toilet by his father. I did know that in a perfect world children need both parents, but at the same time, I knew that none of us lives in a perfect world. What we often forget is that children need quality of parenting not the quantity of parenting! I knew I would survive – so would my son.

Life consists not of holding good cards but in playing those you do hold well. – JOSH BILLINGS

STRUGGLE AS A SINGLE MOTHER

Life was still tough, even without Carl. I felt as I used to in my school days. Because I was very poor at mathematics, I had a strong feeling throughout my primary school days, that if there were no subject like maths, life would be perfect! Then, in secondary school, I could not get a grip of chemistry: and I thought life could be just perfect if there was no boring subject like chemistry! Suddenly I realized that there would always be tough subjects like maths or boring subjects such as chemistry in LIFE! Life was never meant to be perfect! I humbly accepted the reality that the word 'perfect' was only for God! In life we have to take everything with its imperfections; and that's called the art of living! I had not worked for the last two years, as I had decided to stay with Mykey. I got a job in April '93 and left

What if?

Carl in June '93. What I had not realized was that he had not bothered to pay the rent on the council flat we were living in, nor the electricity bill, resulting in a key meter for the electricity. The working of the key meter does not allow you to put in £10 worth of electricity. You can charge the key meter from the different places, like the post office, or corner shops. But the main trauma was the outstanding bill. I had to pay the extra amount towards the unpaid bill before I could get £5 worth of electricity. Only people who have been in that situation can appreciate the feeling of destitution. It was hard! There were times when I had to choose between paying for electricity or food as I could not afford both! And all because of somebody else's mistake. As if I did not have enough to pay for my life's mistakes?

I was fortunate enough to work with nice people in the job centre. My line manager, Wendy Rodger, was a great emotional help. I was totally devastated after receiving the eviction order from the flat. I did not know the law and I was petrified. I was half asleep at work. Wendy reassured me that I would be allowed to stay in the flat. Just tell them the real reason. It was a great relief when the judge said, "We often get scroungers in the court, this is a hardworking mother, who is not denying the responsibility, but can't afford to pay the large outstanding amount." I was delighted that my son, the cat, Kissy and I had a roof over our heads. I had to pay a small amount toward the outstanding debt left by Carl. I think in life we must trust in God to solve our problems, although at times He is late, but there is always a good reason for it. The only problem is that we are unable to see the reasons behind our tests in life.

It was Friday evening, I bought the shopping and at the counter, the bill was too much, but I could not put the shopping back, out of embarrassment, therefore I paid the bill, which resulted in not paying the council rent for that week. I wrote to the council to inform them about the delay. Unfortunately, two days later when I came back from work I noticed that there was no light! The key meter had run out! I had no money, except three pound coins! My salary was monthly, I was shaking with panic. All the food shopping for two weeks would be off! I had no money to pay for the electricity as I had to put in £25 to get £5 worth of electricity. I started to cry while little Mykey kept asking the reason for my tears! I could not put the financial burden or the fault of his father on his tiny shoulders. I told him that my back was hurting.

Mykey was very concerned that there was no light in the flat, but I as soon I lit the candles he was delighted. We ended up having candlelight dinners for days. I was devastated to see the food going off. I asked a few neighbours, but nobody had any space in their fridge to store it. The fire inside my mind was burning faster than anything. I was determined to fight on! Eventually I paid and the light returned to my flat. The same evening I was having a bath and crying over my impoverished state. The bathroom was full of large mirrors, as I loved mirrors. As soon as I finished the bath, I stood up and looked at my nude body. I was thrilled! All my tears dried! My body had power of self-pride because I could not see any bruise on any part of it. I remember I was turning around to check my hips, my back, my breast… I was so happy to see my body without any bruise or scar at least not on the surface! I was determined that I would never allow any man to raise his hand to me again.

'I will survive' was my motto.

Having financial problems is bad, but facing them with kids is real mental torture. Winter was approaching. Mykey was only two and a half years old. I had no money to buy toys for him, but I needed to buy gloves for him. We were in Woolworth's when Mykey picked up a Lego set which was £9:99. I had to distract him, but strong-minded children like Mykey aren't distracted easily. Then I said to him that I only had money for the gloves for him. And he quickly said, "Mykey is not cold, but hungry for Lego." I felt sad for a moment, when I had to take the toy away from my little child's hand and put it back on the shelf. I was about to complain to God when I thought of all those young children in Pakistan who do not even have food to eat: for them eating twice a day was a luxury. I remember, when I was in Pakistan, asking one of the women 'Sabbagi' who used to come to our house to make *chapattis*, how she could afford living? And she said, "We make lentil *dhal* and dip *chapattis* in it, or put salt on *chapattis* and eat." That reminder was enough not to feel sorry for my son.

Christmas came. I knew Carl, being Carl would not send a present for Mykey. I was right to think that way. After Christmas Mykey went back to his nursery and I went back to work. In the evening Mykey was very upset. He kept talking about those children whose Daddies brought them a present. It was sad that he was mentioning details such as his friend's Dad was not living in the same house, but still bought him/her a present. It was heartbreaking to hear him cry for his 'daddy's Christmas present'. I asked him to lie down on my lap. I could see tears rolling down on his cute little cheeks. He then said, "Mum, you can't make people love you! They either do or they don't."

I was amazed at his mature philosophy on life. Well, I suppose hard times mature children faster than we anticipate. I did not want my son to feel sorry for himself. I wanted him to gain experience from losing. I asked him whether he knew the difference between an intelligent boy and a foolish boy? He said, "No."

I had to explain it cruelly that an intelligent boy looks around and sees what God has given him, and is grateful to God: while a silly-billy boy would busy himself finding out what he does not have. There are children who do not even have one parent to love and care for them, there are others in hospital with life-threatening diseases, I had to tell him. "Son, happiness has a limit. There is no limit to misery: always be grateful to God because life always has the potential to get worse."

After leaving Carl, I had to look over my shoulder all the time. Carl had borrowed money for his tools from neighbours. I was in constant terror, as men were constantly coming and shouting to get the money back. I was annoyed with them as well, having to pay for the man who I had kicked out of my life, but I had no choice but to pay the debts off. I knew they were right to demand their money – but not from me.

I knew I had to move away from all these sad memories and start fresh.

Life's a learning circle

Life has taught me some tough lessons. I do hope that my long walk on the road of life can be a guide to others. I would like to share my experience, so that it may help other women.

In many ways, life's journey is similar to driving a car. It is important to look into the rear-view mirror from time to time, but not at the expense of what is happening on the road of life ahead! Also, we should bear in mind that there is no u-turn in this life.

Although life can be a great mentor if one is willing to learn, some of us learn from the mistakes of others. While others are determined to take up the sword and fight the battle themselves, thereby learning the hard way. Yet nobody has the right to judge either category of person. However, there are times in our lives when our wounds can be a source of enlightenment, and thus provide a ray of hope for others. The learning tools are here, whether the reader chooses to learn or not is entirely up to them. I believe that most of our failures in life are not due to a lack of judgment, but a lack of knowledge to rectify those mistakes. We all have to remember that making the wrong choices are simple mistakes of life, although little mistakes of life often lead us to big problems.

However, one has to remember that to make a mistake is human, but to repeat those mistakes is a blunder. Worst of all is to call those mistakes our destiny and to do nothing about them. That is fatal.

RESCUE KIT

Here are few steps for those women who want to pluck up the courage and leave their violent partner.

1: Accept the fact that your partner's violence towards you is not your fault.
2: Do not believe that you are worth nothing! Love and respect yourself.
3: Call the police.
5: Take a grip of your life by LEAVING him.
6: Remember seeing violence is extremely bad for children.
7: Children need quality of parenting, not quantity of parenting.
8: Do not live in belief that HE WILL CHANGE. Face reality and leave him today.
9: Violent relationships only get worse with time.
10: There are places such as women's refuge for shelter. Contact:
    Domestic Violence Crisis Line – 0870 599 5443
    Shelter Line – 0808 800 4444
    Women's Aid – 0808 200 0247 www.womensaid.org.uk
11: Have a separate account and save some money.
12: Leave when they are away from house.
13: Don't take things with you, keep your safety and children's safety paramount.
13: Take your children with you; however do not tell them the plan.
14: REBUILD your life; we only live once.

WHAT IF?

Asma Pumpi Moore on receiving her Degree with son Mykey

CHAPTER NINE

THE END JUSTIFIES THE MEANS

Life has taught me many lessons, but at a very high price. My faith in God gave me tremendous strength to fight my battles, from the emotional heat of the Eastern culture to the cold solitude of Western un-civilization.

It was my firm believe in God, the source of wisdom and knowledge, which prevented me from believing and obeying some of the man-made, despicable rules in the Islamic society. I accepted the challenges that were thrown at me by life. However, in the process, there were times when I felt I was attending my own funeral, but then again as I discovered myself I was re-born!

To find yourself is the shortest route to finding God! – APM

FAILURE TEACHES SUCCESS!

I fought all my battles, with great courage and in the belief that one day God would reward me. That moment arrived in July 1999. When my name *"Asma Pumpi Moore!"* was called in the Middlesex University, I was overwhelmed to receive a British Law Degree! It was like giving birth to another child! After an intensive, three-year-long labour.

My son Mykey, aged 8 years, shouted from the crowd, 'Well done, Mum!'

"If we believe in God, then nothing is impossible."